WHY PUT A BOW TIE ON A LLAMA?

How a crazy idea can change your life and transform your business

Celia Gaze

First published in Great Britain by Practical Inspiration Publishing, 2020

ISBN   978-1-78860-124-5 (print)
        978-1-78860-126-9 (epub)
        978-1-78860-125-2 (mobi)

Front cover image by Alice May: www.alicemay.weebly.com
Back cover image by Chris McGloin Photography: chrismcgloinphotography.com

Practical Inspiration
PUBLISHING

This book has been written for my son Matthew (aged 11). I started this journey when you were a baby and now you've just started secondary school. I hope that by reading this book, you will understand why you visited so many places with me and I would love it if this book inspired you to make the most of your life, too.

Praise

A fascinating rollercoaster ride of a book detailing the ups and downs of setting up a wedding events business in rural Lancashire. From the painful process of dealing with red tape and bureaucracy, through to handling a unique building programme, then marketing, staffing and sculpting the business – this book covers it all in an easy-to-understand, practical and very real way. As a Glamping site owner also in the North West, I could really relate to this book in a way you can't with most. It was full of real-world examples of how hard business can be at times and a very honest insight for anyone looking to diversify their farm. There's very little information out there about this and I would like to thank Celia for taking the time to share her vast experience. I'm sure that reading the book will give you some real light bulb moments and plenty of takeaways for you to implement in your own business. This rollercoaster ride is a must read for anyone looking to set up any type of leisure business, or those already in it.

Alex Young, Campsite Manager,
Stanley Villa Farm Camping, Preston, Lancashire

Despite every barrier you can imagine being put in her way, Celia Gaze shows how you can transform a rundown farm into a thriving rural business. Learn from her mistakes, but more importantly learn from her success, tenacity and vision. Celia is a force of nature and her book reflects that in every page.

Christine Nicolson, The Profit Fixer

This book is a very useful guide for anyone thinking of converting their home or farm into a venue for public use. It documents Celia's journey, the challenges she faced and conquered and what she learned along the way. As soon as you have a gem of an idea to create a unique wedding venue on your private property, read this book. It will make your journey easier and help you to develop your processes, identify the external support and ensure you build your resilience to be successful.

Jacinta Scannell, Managing Director,
The Conference Collective Limited

This is a fantastic read to learn the ups and downs, do's and don'ts of starting and setting up a business. A must have for anyone wanting to start up a business.

Jacqui Mann, Founder and Managing Director, J Mann
Associates and author of Recruit, Inspire & Retain: How
to Create a Company Culture to Grow Your Business

Celia's story is so inspiring and truthfully told. She has faced many challenges on her journey of building a business and talks about things that may people keep hidden. Talking about the challenges inspires others and let's them know that they are not alone when things don't quite go to plan. In this book Celia proves that with commitment, clarity and the ability to pivot when something goes wrong, your crazy business idea can become a reality. I have loved seeing Celia on her journey to success and know that there is still a lot more to come – she really is an inspirational woman and her success with no doubt inspire you to push the boundaries of what you think is possible and stand with her on that journey to success. Having visited the farm, I can confirm it is truly magical and Celia and her team have done such an amazing job!

Emma Etheridge, The Wedding Biz Coach and
Founder of The Wedding Biz Club

Foreword

Big transformations and life-changing stories are meant to happen in Los Angeles, not Lancashire.

They happen to other people. Not to us.

And when the star tells their story they usually 'polish' it. They hide what really happened behind a veneer that makes them look like a genius. But that's not real.

The story you hold in your hands right now is real.

It didn't happen in Hollywood. It happened in Turton, Lancashire. On the moors. In an old sheep farm.

But it's real. Very real. And there's no polish or veneer.

I first met Celia over four years ago and I've been privileged to have a ringside seat for the story you're about to read.

And read it you must.

Because it's a remarkable story packed with nuggets of gold for anyone with aspirations to bring about a change in their business. Or a change in their life.

Celia's honesty and 'no-holds-barred' account of how she transformed a run-down hill farm into one of the country's most sought after wedding venues is both inspiring and bloody useful for anyone who'd like their business – or their life – to be in a different place.

You know, long ago I realised that success leaves clues. That people who achieve remarkable things do specific things to achieve those results.

As well as being a fine story this book leaves a lot of clues.

In many ways it's really a blueprint.

A road map.

A journey that we too can go on with our businesses now that Celia has shown us the way...

Nigel Botterill
Founder and Chief Executive, the Entrepreneurs Circle

Preface

I am there sat at the tribunal. Nobody had warned me what a tribunal would be like. It felt like a court. I didn't realise there would be an audience listening to my every word. I felt judged, overwhelmed and worried sick.

Despite so much work to prepare for this day and having Stephen and Edward at my side, I felt inadequate in the face of the suit-wearing lady laden with files of evidence against me.

All I had tried to do was to create my own business, by turning a neglected farm into something special, something amazing – to follow my dreams.

Nobody had really explained about what it's like to face potential bankruptcy and to have staff accountable and depending on you. The stress I faced as an NHS Director was nothing compared to the stress you face when you have bills to pay. People with mortgages and families are relying on you and you have no bookings and no money – what on earth do you do? I just didn't understand VAT and business rates.

Nobody warned me that when you become successful, people swarm on you like vultures circling overhead, wanting every bit of you. Were these people there at the beginning? No, they thought your idea was stupid, crazy

– why on earth would you invest in llamas? What on earth is that going to do for you?

I had no idea about the road ahead and all the problems I would face when I set up the business. If somebody had drawn me a road map to follow, which could have pre-warned me about the potential problems I would face, it would have been so helpful.

That is the purpose of this book.

Why put a bow tie on a llama?

The 'bow tie on a llama' represents a turning point in my business; some people would call it the tipping point. It's something that happens unexpectedly but goes on to completely change and transform both your business and your life.

The day I put a bow tie on a llama was the day that transformed everything. The minute I put the bow tie on the llama, my business became different. We leapt from 15 to 43 weddings in one year (2016) and we continued to grow. That was the start of the transformation of my business. Up to that point, The Wellbeing Farm was just another venue, but the bow-tie-wearing llamas meant we suddenly became a venue that stood out.

Figure 0.1: A couple of our bow-tie-wearing llamas
(Photo credit: David Lake Photography)

Acknowledgements

The most special mention must go to my partner, Stephen – you are my rock, my constant source of support and I could never have done any of this without you. From letting me just transform your farm to your constant support, being by my side while I went through so many awful experiences, setting up a business tests the strongest of relationships and I thank you for the support you have given me.

Next in line to thank must be my mum (Heather) – she is my best friend, my confidante, she is a huge influence in my life and her fantastic personality, enthusiasm for life and infectious ability to tell stories have definitely made me the person that I am today. She always makes me laugh and we don't just laugh, but we laugh and laugh until there is a silence between us. I laugh till I almost can't breathe. And we laugh until both of us literally have tears streaming down our faces. You have been an amazing source of support to me and I don't think I would have coped without you.

Family forms a huge part in the type of person you become. I'd like to thank my dad for his gifts of learning and getting up early in the morning, and especially for leaving his bag of bow ties. A special mention goes to my brothers and sisters – I wouldn't be the person I am without your support and love. A very special thank you must go to my brother Harry. Your vision and design skills and the physical work you put into transforming an old agricultural building into a wedding barn that makes everyone say WOW when they walk through the doors is testimony to your design and construction talent which deserves recognition.

A huge thank you goes also to Edward for his patience, sound advice and support. Love and thanks must also go to the Whitehead family, in particular to David for his invaluable farming advice and help, and to Dave Grundy for his building knowledge and expertise – thank you for making me feel so welcome and for the support you have provided during my journey to transform Wheatsheaf Hill Farm.

I can't thank Victor Giannandrea, my mentor, enough – you are the person who has done more to help me develop the business than anyone (apart from Stephen loaning me his farm of course) and I am so incredibly grateful for how you have helped me and for the time, patience, encouragement, help, support, experience and guidance you have given me.

Huge thanks must go to all the staff and volunteers – past and present. I could never have done this without each and every one of you and you've all played a huge role in transforming the business into what it is today. I love the laughs we've had; the journey that we've been on and your personalities have given the farm the reputation it has today. A very special thanks must go to Harry Bithell for everything he has done to help me.

My business story has been shaped and supported by so many people who deserve thanks.

I'd like to thank the following people for helping me with my planning application: Kathryn Jukes, Gary Hoerty, John Welbank, Councillors Jean and Colin Rigby, and Brian Bailey.

Thank you to Rick Patterson, Philip Ambler, Paul Guinan, Philip Harrison and Prakash Patel for your support in gaining funding and overcoming regulations.

To the builders who have worked non-stop to transform the farm – especially Alan, Fraser and Chris.

To the many people who shaped my service offer, with a special thank you to Mike Harrison who provided a massive source of support when I was setting up the farm – I will always be incredibly grateful to you for that. Also to Justine Forrest for the support you gave me with the cookery school classes. Finally to Sara Lobley for her immense help and advice when we first started weddings at the farm.

To Martin my accountant, thank you for the help you have given me and allowing me to enjoy finance again!

I'd like to thank Jessica Pendlebury for the images in the book and Alice May for the picture of the llama for my cover design. I'd also like to give a special thanks to Nikki Barlow for all the support she has provided in developing my website and to Chris McGloin for the creation of that amazing video which put The Wellbeing Farm on the map.

I've been lucky to be a member of the Entrepreneurs Circle for over three years now and I've got to say that I have learned more about sales and marketing from Nigel Botterill (the Chief Executive and Founder of the Entrepreneurs Circle) than I learned from my MBA!

A heartfelt thank you to the numerous wedding suppliers for supporting the farm and being part of our transformational journey. A special thanks must go to the photographers and videographers who share their incredible images and films with us and have helped us put The Wellbeing Farm on the map.

Finally a huge thank you must go to Alison Jones at Practical Inspiration, whose 10 Day Book Proposal Challenge helped me enormously in pulling this book together and whose guidance has been invaluable. Mention must also be made of the team at Newgen Publishing UK for their fantastic editing of the book.

I am incredibly lucky to have created a business which I absolutely love; however this business would not exist if it wasn't for the amazing couples we meet every day and the amazing weddings and events we experience. There are so many occasions and memories I could talk about, but a few are magical and I thought you might enjoy these story snippets.

One of the funniest moments was when we were asked by a couple (Jake and Lana) if they could have a karate fight as their first dance! I thought I had experienced most things associated with weddings, but when you see a bride in her dress taking part in a karate fight on her wedding day you've seen it all...

A magical moment was when I took a phone call from someone who wanted to propose to his girlfriend in a helicopter and then land at the farm for a vintage afternoon tea – such an amazing, magical moment when that helicopter landed!

One of my proudest moments was to help a dying man's wish come true – to marry the love of his life at the farm literally two days before he passed away.

So a final thank you to everyone who has made me laugh, encouraged me in my journey and taught me something useful. Your input has made me a better person.

My story

What and who has shaped me to be the creative and enthusiastic person I have become? I want to give you a brief background to my life. This background gave me skills in resilience, entrepreneurship and a fighting spirit. I also explain here how stress and corporate burnout made me resign from the NHS which I loved and how I found the farm.

Family shapes your life – I got my passion for learning from my dad, who is highly educated, and my enthusiasm and personality from my mum, who is the heart and soul of my family. I also attribute my personality, mannerisms and stoicism to my Grandpa Richardson, who fought colon cancer at an early age and was such an inspiration, and finally I believe I get my fighting spirit and zest for life from my Grandma Richardson, who lived until she was over 100 years of age and even went down a helter skelter aged 90 – she was that type of woman!

My competitiveness is thanks to my brothers and sisters – as a child I always loved cooking, organising shows and, being one of six, was the child who was bossy and always had to organise everything, so I was creative from an early age.

Figure 0.2: Celia aged 13 as a North West Finalist of
Junior Cook of the Year

I didn't enjoy school and to be honest wasn't
particularly encouraged by my teachers, so my exam
results weren't brilliant. I went to Blackpool College
where instead of A-levels I did a Diploma in Hotel,
Catering and Institutional Operations. After graduating
from college I went to study for a degree in Hotel and
Catering Management at North London Polytechnic,
now known as the University of North London.

My third year of university was a placement year in which we had to seek work experience. I wrote to the Managing Director of The Garrick Club (a prestigious London-based gentleman's club) asking them if I could become their Management Trainee. I got the job and just loved it. The only problem was that on a day-to-day basis I struggled to recognise people. Sometimes I would be talking to famous people you see on the television every day and I didn't even know who they were! I gained fantastic experience in hospitality and organising events – there was one time when I was asked to organise the Christmas party for children of Garrick Club members. The members were downstairs in the main room and I had to entertain the children in the room above them. I remember my enthusiasm got the better of me and the members came upstairs to report that never before in the history of The Garrick Club had the ceilings ever shaken!

I finished my final year at university and returned home to Preston. I applied for over 100 student graduate positions and spent my summer doing nothing but attending interviews, receiving piles and piles of rejections. In desperation, my mum rang the local hospital and asked them whether I could come and do some voluntary work for them. I joined the NHS as a volunteer trainee manager and was exposed to every area within the hospital, spending time circulating between 62 different departments from theatres to administration and I loved it.

As working in the hospital was a voluntary position, I needed some income – this was the start of my entrepreneurial spirit as I used to go to jumble sales on a Saturday to find quality clothes. I would wash and iron the clothes on Saturday afternoons, putting them all on hangers with a plastic covering, and sell them for three to four times the price at a car boot sale the next day.

I gained enough experience and understanding of the NHS that I was offered an administration role, which then led to me being offered the role of Assistant Practice Manager at a GP surgery. Over the next five years I fluctuated between holding management positions in general practice (primary care) and in hospitals (secondary care) and I also gained my Master of Business Administration (MBA) and qualifications in project management. It was unusual for someone to have experience in both primary and secondary care, so I had carved a nice niche out for myself. This experience resulted in me securing a role as Director of Service Reconfiguration, leading a big consultation process to design and reconfigure NHS services across four hospitals within six towns.

For the role I moved from London up to Edgworth, a small village nestled in between Blackburn and Bolton – a far cry from living in Central London. One day someone I worked with invited me to attend the local pub quiz. It was at the quiz that I met Stephen – now my partner.

Stephen was always quite shy, so it was a few weeks before he plucked up the courage to ask me on a date.

The thing I liked about Stephen from the beginning was that he didn't try to impress anyone. He was a local butcher. He was just so grounded and secure. Stephen's demeanour was calming – I've always been a complete stress-head who is overly enthusiastic, outgoing and ambitious, and Stephen was so secure and so stable. We were complete opposites, but we just clicked.

Our first date was for a meal at The Toby, a restaurant on the moors near Edgworth. The journey from The Toby to Stephen's home was obviously along country roads which were pitch black – I had no idea Stephen owned a farm until I visited it and eventually saw it in daylight. It had a number of stables, but the grounds had been neglected. Stephen had inherited the farm from his Uncle Tom, a really lovely man. But there had not been much investment in the farm aside from the livery yard.

The Director of Reconfiguration role required me to manage a complicated, political project, essential to which was securing leadership and input from clinicians around the design of future health services for the area and then winning the hearts and minds of the public in the form of a big public consultation. At the time, I organised a huge workshop in Manchester to discuss the consultation; the event was facilitated by a former BBC presenter who pulled me to one side and said, 'What on earth are you doing in the NHS? Your skills are far more suited to a commercial environment.' I thought nothing of it at the time, but I think he planted a seed. He planted the seed which grew into the idea of creating my own business.

At this point, I had a job I absolutely loved – I was ambitious and wanted to progress up the NHS career path. The consultation and decision ended up being challenged by a local MP and I had to go to the High Court of London to fight a judicial review, which I won. It was around this time that I discovered I was pregnant. Having experienced two miscarriages, I was desperate to have a baby, so the timing was perfect. I had completed the project to deliver the consultation on the reconfiguration of health services and my position of leading the consultation was being made redundant, so I took maternity leave.

I was enjoying maternity leave when I got the phone call – Celia what are you doing at the moment? Would you be interested in a turnaround role? How could I resist...

Contents

Introduction

Have you ever thought, 'Is this my life?' Have you ever imagined you're lying on your death bed and looking back wondering, 'What did I do with my life? How many people will be at my funeral? What will I have achieved?'

I often wonder this – perhaps I have an in-built fear of not making the most of my life, and if this is a fear that you experience, then I hope you will find solace in what I have written. It's a guide to making the most of your life and I want to share my story with you. I hope that how I went from a stressed-out NHS Director to the Managing Director of a multi-award-winning quirky wedding venue with bow-tie-wearing llamas and the lessons I learned along the way will help you follow my lead and translate your own 'crazy' idea into a personal and business success.

1

Sometimes I look back as I gaze out of the window at the farm and I just think 'WOW'.

So who have I written this book for?

- **Wannabe business owners.** Maybe you are fed up and frustrated with your job and you'd love the freedom to be a business owner/entrepreneur. Perhaps you already have an idea about starting a business and you need some guidance on how to test your idea and implement it.

- **Business owners.** Maybe you are a business owner and your business just isn't unique enough – it's not standing out from a crowded marketplace and you are looking for help and creative ways to achieve this.

- **Facing a mid-life or quarter-life crisis.** Could it be that you are fed up with your work and reflecting on your career so far – you want more out of your life but you are wondering what on earth you can do?

- **Supplier in the wedding or hospitality industry.** Maybe you are a supplier that wants to grow your business and are searching for inspiration.

- **Farmer/land-owner.** Perhaps you are a farmer and are looking for ways to diversify your farm – you're looking into whether hosting weddings could be the answer, but you aren't sure where to start.

What you've all got in common is a crazy idea. If you have that idea, don't let anyone stop you; take the gamble.

You only have one life, don't waste it all thinking 'What if?' Live your life now and give it a go – what have you got to lose?

How to use this book and the support available

Over the past eight years I have worked hard to transform Wheatsheaf Hill Farm into the business it is today. I have overcome barriers and obstacles, removed blockages to progress, dealt with all sorts of situations and worked with lots of different characters. I am grateful for all the failures, barriers, blockages and bureaucracy I faced, as they've given me a wealth of experience and taught me valuable life lessons. Throughout this book I document my story and the experiences I went through and reflect on the lessons I have learned to help you to think about the steps and action you can take and use the information to learn more. The book is supported by a website (www.celiagaze. com) where you can find further information to help you.

PART ONE

**Getting established –
planning your business and
transforming your venue**

Chapter 1

What happens to you to make you want to change your life?

Never underestimate the power you have to take your
life in a new direction.

Germany Kent

In this chapter I describe the circumstances which led
me to leave a career I loved and to rethink my life.

I'm driving to work, and my knuckles are going white
with the tension on the steering wheel. I can almost feel
the tightness in my heart – there's tingling going down
my arm – and I'm thinking, oh my goodness, I am not
even 40 and I'm having a heart attack. I dreaded going
into work. I was feeling sick. And I just didn't know what
was happening to me.

I arrived that morning, and it was a Director's
meeting. A Director's meeting to discuss the performance
of the turnaround projects that I was the Director for.
You see, in this role in the NHS, I was the Turnaround
Director. Turnaround Director meant going in to help an
organisation save money and actually turn it around. This

was fundamental – I had to save around £42 million and I had been given months to do it.

It wasn't turning around. Looking back, I was unbelievably stressed; I felt I was slowly drowning, I didn't understand all the figures, I couldn't get useful information out of anyone and I was out of my depth.

It was stress beyond anything I could imagine. At the time I didn't know anything about stress. I'd had stressful projects in the past, I'd had demanding, busy projects, I'd had projects that were high profile, and I'd even won a judicial review against an MP in the High Court in London.

I wasn't scared of big projects, big decisions, big things in life or anything like that. But when I encountered this, it wasn't so much the role or the task that had to be done. It was my imagination, the sideways glances, the hidden criticism, believing others thought that I should not have returned after having a baby. It was this snide criticism saying, 'She's lost her touch. She's not that good. What happened to her?'

It was the challenge to my favoured way of working. My pre-baby 4am start days were brilliant – I could always achieve so much. But with a baby, he wanted to wake up at 4am too. The golden hours that I'd so cherished before were now spent breast-feeding my baby. I'd gone back to work far too soon. You see, I was enjoying maternity leave when I got the phone call – Celia what are you doing at the moment? Would you be interested in a turnaround role? How could I resist…

I was driving into work, dreading this meeting. I parked some distance away to fit in some exercise. As I walked through the foot tunnel, I thought, 'I'm feeling really ill.' I arrived at the meeting and began to present the figures that showed how the situation wasn't turning around, it was actually getting worse. I was challenged on the figures and my report was being pulled apart. I felt so ill I had to walk out. I have never, ever in my life walked out of a meeting.

I didn't know it at the time, but usually as part of a turnaround things get worse before they get better. At the time though, I blamed myself; I blamed myself that I wasn't good enough to turn this organisation around. How on earth could one person turn around a £42 million project, anyway? But I took it upon myself. I took it personally. I'd been appointed; I'd been chosen to be this Turnaround Director. I thought of myself as a bit of a knight in shining armour. I could save these organisations. I could do this. But I couldn't.

This moment had been building up. A sign of stress is when you start thinking that everyone is criticising you and that everybody is against you. You think they perceive you as a complete and utter failure. I was crying all the time. I just couldn't reduce the deficit.

I hadn't been sleeping – I just couldn't. I felt as though my head was in some sort of fuzzy cloud – this was stress.

I remember someone suggesting that perhaps I should go and see a doctor. My initial response was silly when I look back. I didn't want stress to be on my medical records and the thought of going to a doctor to admit that there was something wrong, why I couldn't talk, why I couldn't think, why I couldn't deal with this, was really embarrassing.

I remember going to see the doctor, and I sat down with him and I described everything that I'd been going through. I told him about the things I had been feeling and experiencing and how I felt such a failure. I told him everyone was against me. I told him about this constant fuzz, this constant cloudiness in my brain.

He paused and said something which stopped me in my stride. He said, 'You are going to be very ill.' My response was 'What on earth are you talking about?' He replied, 'You're having a breakdown.' He went on to say, 'You've got to stop and you've got to take some time off.'

My initial response was shock – I even challenged him: 'What on earth are you talking about? I can't possibly take time off because I'm too busy. I've got so much work to do, I just can't stop.' He said, 'If you don't stop, you're going to be very ill.' This shook me into action. I took his advice and said, 'Okay, I'll have a week off.' He replied, 'I am signing you off for a minimum of two weeks.'

I had those two weeks off and I booked myself in to see a counsellor privately. I don't know if you have experienced stress or corporate burnout? You may have picked this book up because of its link to stress. If you have, you'll understand what I'm now about to say.

You feel so embarrassed about what will happen. You know you have this reputation as a high-flying, career-driven, ambitious person. You are not known to be a crying, weak person. But this is what overwork and stress does to you. These are the symptoms of corporate burnout. I thought I was a failure, but it was an impossible situation that I'd been put under. I should never have been approached when I was on maternity leave. I should have demanded that I was given a decent team around me to make this project happen.

Two weeks pass quickly and at the end of the two weeks I was dreading going back to work. I felt absolutely sick, and I thought, 'Why am I doing this to myself? I'm not going to go back to this organisation which is going to make me ill.' Which was ironic considering it was the NHS.

I decided that my health and my baby were more important to me than this ambition. I resigned. I subsequently had a lot of counselling – I will admit that it was a massive blow to my ego that I couldn't deliver this. But what did happen, and what was helpful, is that the top person who heads up turnaround in the NHS met with me and said that he had worked with many experienced Turnaround Directors in the private and public sectors in his role and that there are hardly any that would have taken on this project.

He went on to say that the fact I had had a go and tried was commendation in itself. He explained that in his experience, 'It was not an easy turnaround, and not many people would have been able to do it.' I had just gone one step too far.

So I had to pick up my life, and there I was, having been a massively career-driven ambitious person who loved her work so much. Now I was effectively out of a job, suffering from corporate burnout, and wondering what on earth I was going to do next.

Over to you...

- What are the circumstances that are making you reflect on your life?
- Have you ever experienced stress, corporate burnout or something similar? Is this the reason you want to change your life?

Chapter 2

What's the crazy idea?

I did decide that the world is made up of crazy ideas. History is one long processional of crazy ideas. The things I loved most – books, sports, democracy, free enterprise – started as crazy ideas.

P. Knight, *Shoe Dog: A Memoir by the Creator of Nike* (2016)

In this chapter I describe how I came up with the idea for the business and the circumstances which made me put a bow tie on a llama.

I had Matthew (my baby) whom I absolutely loved, obviously, but – you may think this is selfish – Matthew wasn't enough. I wanted other things. I was never really geared up for being a full-time mum; I wanted to do other things with my life.

I've always loved going on courses. The funniest moment I experienced on a course was when I thought I had booked onto a 'how to become a magician' course. I turned up a few minutes late so I missed the introduction to the course. When I arrived, they were dimming the lights and I thought we were going to be taught a magical illusion. This went on for quite a while and there didn't seem to be much magic appearing, so I turned to the next person and whispered, 'When do you think they'll start teaching us the magic trick?' The other person looked at me in horror, so I asked, 'This is the "how to become a magician course" isn't it?' and he responded, 'No, it's the "how to connect with the dead course".' I've never got out of a class so quickly!

My philosophy is to make the most of your life and have no regrets. I love learning. I am absolutely addicted to reading. I try to read a book a week. I've been on well over 100 courses. So, it's no surprise that one day in South Manchester I found myself on a giftwrapping course. I was there, having a day off, with Matthew being looked after by my mum. While on that course, I overheard two ladies talking about the courses that they were running from their house that weekend. I was trying to wrap my gift, while leaning over to earwig on their conversation and feeling envious about how excited they were about the courses they were going to run at the weekend. I listened while they explained how they were going to plan them, how they were getting ideas from this course, what food they were going to serve, how they were going to do it. I was listening so intently it almost became a bit embarrassing, as I leaned too far and nearly squashed their gift wrapping.

It suddenly dawned on me, 'Why don't I set up my own courses?' I absolutely love doing courses; why couldn't I do that with Stephen's farm? I could transform it into something really special. I couldn't get home quickly enough.

I remember driving home, thinking, 'How am I going to approach Stephen with this idea?' I've never been subtle, so I just walked in and said, 'I've been thinking I could do something with your farm. I've got a bit of an idea, would you let me?' This is another thing I love about Stephen, as he just responded saying 'Yeah, why not?' There was no questioning, there was no 'Oh, what are you going to do? What are you thinking of?'

So, from that moment, while looking after Matthew at home, I started doing research. I became obsessed with stress – what was this condition that had turned me from this high-flying, ambitious, enthusiastic individual, to a crumbling wreck reduced to tears by the slightest bit of criticism.

I read every book there was on stress. I went online for hours trying to find an answer to what it was all about. I even enrolled on a stress management course and achieved a qualification in stress management. I then went on to receive a qualification in organisational stress management. I was delighted to be sent a personal letter from the course director, who wrote to tell me that I had passed with distinction, a rare honour.

One of the modules on the course was about creating an environment which enabled you to live stress-free. I decided to base my coursework on the perfect vision of a business that would help individuals be as stress-free as possible. At the time (2008), stress and wellbeing was an emerging trend but was not as recognised as it is now. I looked at all of the ways to improve someone's wellbeing, and started thinking I could apply the Five Ways to Mental Wellbeing model to a business.[1]

These five activities seemed to be at the heart of my decision to change my life. I realised that if you followed these five principles, they were critical to getting a grip on your life and starting to live it.

Five Ways to Wellbeing
Connect...
Be active...
Take notice...
Keep learning...
Give...

I questioned what could I do from the farm that would help people's wellbeing and I used this framework to transform the farm and to create this perfect visitor experience purposely designed to help their wellbeing. This is how I came up with the name of the business – The Wellbeing Farm.

---

[1] New Economics Foundation, *Five Ways to Mental Wellbeing* (2008).

Connect...

With the people around you. With family, friends, colleagues and neighbours. At home, work, school or in your local community. Think of these as the cornerstones of your life and invest time in developing them. Building these connections will support and enrich you every day.[2]

Applying this concept I decided to run events like meditation courses; I also had the idea of turning the upper level of the main barn into meeting rooms for companies to hire for corporate events, using the fields for activities such as It's a Knockout®, archery and team building exercises in a non-stuffy, non-corporate environment.

Over to you...

- How do you connect with people?
- What do your family, friends and colleagues think of your decision to change your life? Have you discussed it with them?
- Your decision to change your life will have a huge impact on your family and friends and you need to be prepared for that.

---

[2] New Economics Foundation, *Five Ways to Mental Wellbeing*.

19

Be active…

Go for a walk or run. Step outside. Cycle. Play a game. Garden. Dance. Exercising makes you feel good. Most importantly, discover a physical activity you enjoy and that suits your level of mobility and fitness.[3]

The farm was a livery yard with lots of stables. I knew I didn't want horses there, so I decided to do some research on what other types of animal might use a stable. I came across the concept of llama trekking as a way to reduce stress. Llamas seemed to tick every box, including the 'Be active' box.

Over to you…

- As you will find out later on in this book, health is even more critical than ever for an entrepreneur. How active are you?
- Is health a priority in your life?
- How balanced is your life?

---

[3] New Economics Foundation, *Five Ways to Mental Wellbeing*.

Take notice...

Be curious. Catch sight of the beautiful. Remark on the unusual. Notice the changing seasons. Savour the moment, whether you are walking to work, eating lunch or talking to friends. Be aware of the world around you and what you are feeling. Reflecting on your experiences will help you appreciate what matters to you.[4]

The farm's situation in the countryside was perfect for this, and enjoying a position 800 ft above sea level meant that we had amazing views for ticking this box.

Over to you...

- How do you take notice?
- Are you aware of the environment around you or of your home life?
- What can you do to step back, observe and reflect?
- As an exercise, to help you appreciate the people with whom you work, make a mental decision to look tomorrow for a particular behaviour or a particular action that you are then going to reward

---

[4] New Economics Foundation, *Five Ways to Mental Wellbeing*.

with a 'thank you!' or a pat on the back. In my own context, thinking about kinds of behaviour at work is useful as part of taking notice, as is rewarding that behaviour to show that you have noticed it.

Keep learning...

Try something new. Rediscover an old interest. Sign up for that course. Take on a different responsibility at work. Fix a bike. Learn to play an instrument or how to cook your favourite food. Set a challenge you will enjoy achieving. Learning new things will make you more confident as well as being fun.[5]

I could incorporate my love of courses with other elements. Stephen's family had run Whitehead's Butchers for generations (they've been trading for over 130 years) so I thought Stephen could do butchery courses from the farm. This idea expanded into setting up a cookery school.

---

[5] New Economics Foundation, *Five Ways to Mental Wellbeing*.

Over to you...

- How much time do you spend learning?
- Have you been and visited other businesses to get ideas?
- Are you reading books?
- Are you attending conferences or participating in online learning to expand your knowledge?

Give...

Do something nice for a friend, or a stranger. Thank someone. Smile. Volunteer your time. Join a community group. Look out, as well as in. Seeing yourself, and your happiness, linked to the wider community can be incredibly rewarding and creates connections with the people around you.[6]

We could make sure that the business was sustainable from the outset in terms of building materials, ethos and culture to create a caring environment. We could run school visits for children to learn about sustainability and where food comes from, incorporating farming and education.

---

[6] New Economics Foundation, *Five Ways to Mental Wellbeing*.

Over to you…

- Sustainability is a huge issue at the moment – have you considered this within your business?
- What could you give back to the community? Is this in your business plan?

I started travelling around the country with Matthew in tow undertaking primary research. I visited 196 venues all around the country from Devon to Scotland, and every time I visited a different venue I got ideas.

All these ideas were amassed into this huge disparate business plan and proposal. Remember that I came from an NHS background, where huge proposals were the norm. People prepared these massive proposals and business cases with huge amounts of evidence – after all, it was publicly funded.

I presented my plan to Stephen. 'I think I could turn your farm into a venue for courses – we could do cookery, butchery, and we could also do meetings and corporate events.' I involved the services of Business Link, which was a national network of business support agencies managed by the Small Business Service, a government agency set up to champion small businesses. An advisor from Business Link helped me assemble all my ideas into a five-year business plan. The original business plan can be viewed on my website (www.celiagaze.com).

Over to you...

- Has my story sparked something in you...?
- What has prompted your interest in changing your life?
- Have you discovered anything which makes you want to change?
- What ideas do you have for your business?
- How do you want to transform your business?

Chapter 3

How do you begin to transform your premises?

Obstacles don't have to stop you. If you run into a wall, don't turn around and give up. Figure out how to climb it, go through it, or work around it.

Michael Jordan

This chapter is obviously highly relevant if you are a land-owner or farmer and are thinking about how to transform your premises. In this chapter I cover how I transformed a neglected, run-down farm into a multi-award-winning venue. For other readers, it will cover the bureaucracy and frustration involved in setting up a business and how I have had my traits of perseverance and resilience tested to the extreme.

I have been very lucky because Stephen had the perfect premises to transform.

One of my biggest mistakes is that, in hindsight, I should have tested the water before embarking on the huge transformation process that I undertook. You see, I didn't test anything before hand – yes, I'd done loads of research, toured 196 venues to get ideas etc. – but I'd actually never run a venue personally, never managed a building project and never run a farm.

There was no book or manual to tell you how to transform a farm into a venue, and I didn't have any experience of planning permission, dealing with architects, gaining Building Regulations approval, licensing your premises or anything else. Everything I write about below I had to find out personally – the hard way – through hours and hours of research and by making mistakes. I'm hoping that by documenting my learning, and writing this book, you can learn from my errors.

I have consolidated my learning into a series of drivers for you to consider and think about as you transform your premises.

The first thing I recommend is to be really clear on your customer audience – what sort of customers you will serve and what they want. This is known as developing your customer avatar. Experimentation, testing and piloting is essential before embarking on any transformation of your buildings.

You don't have to have a full-blown farm to start with – you just need 2–3 acres of land. You could use an outdoor location such as a large garden, a field or even some rented land and try your idea out. Obviously you'll have to do some research as to whether you can hold events on the land: speak to the neighbours and obtain a temporary events licence from the Council. What I'm suggesting is that you don't have to completely rebuild a farm like I did. Start off by experimenting and testing the market – you can begin by hiring a marquee or tipi in a field and hiring toilets, chairs/tables etc., using outside caters and an outside bar service, and setting aside an area of land for car parking. Test the market and establish demand.

I unfortunately didn't experiment or start small at all…

Over to you…

- I would highly recommend starting small and learning the lessons as you go on.
- When you have tested the market and learned some lessons, then you can grow.
- You can start thinking about transforming the buildings when you have a proven business model.
- Engage the services of your planning authority early on, tell them you are thinking of buying a property to transform into a venue and they will tell you the requirements.
- Look to find out the local rules and regulations and do your homework as you search for the property.

Designing your premises and vision

You will read in the next section about the problems and frustrations I experienced obtaining planning permission. When I submitted the original plans to the planning authority and outlined what I wanted to do with the farm, it was met with outright rejection – in hindsight this was probably to do with the fact that I hadn't tested the market and there was no proven business model. As a result of the outright rejection, I had to adapt my building design to fit the original footprint of the farm buildings to stand any chance of being granted planning permission, which did restrict my vision for the business. I was also conscious of not spending too much money on architects at this stage as I was wary of future rejection by the planning authority and then everything I had invested may never have come to fruition.

So when I look back at how I designed the farm, I made mistakes. I found an architect on the back of free architecture support called 'Architect in the House' which was a scheme run by Shelter, the housing and homelessness charity, and the Royal Institute of British Architects (RIBA). The scheme matched homeowners with a local RIBA chartered architect who gives up an hour of their time for a design consultation. As I had experienced so many problems with planning permission and they weren't allowing me to radically change the size of the original premises, I couldn't really do much to change the outside of the building, so the advice I was after related to the inside of the building. The plan was to convert the barn and stable block into a facility for corporate events, day courses, cookery demonstrations and llama trekking in Edgworth. I wanted architectural advice on the best internal layout for the purposes of the proposed facility.

If I knew then what I know now, I would never have converted the main farm building. I would have just converted the large agricultural barn – this would have been a lot cheaper and would have saved so much money, time and heartache. This is the purpose of this book – to explain my mistakes so you don't make them too.

Over to you...

- You need to be really clear about your target customer and their wants and desires from a facility. This is where the work you do on your customer avatar at the outset is critical.
- Start simple, prove that your business model will work (for example, by starting off with tents or marquees on your land to try your idea out and test the market), prove the demand for the business and then start to change your buildings.

- Visit as many premises as you can to seek ideas and how they operate. This will also help you in developing your business case as you can see the impact that other developments have had on their local area.
- Look objectively at your farm/premises and seek early engagement, preferably from an architect with experience of farm diversification. Architects with this experience are a lot more prevalent than there were eight years ago.
- Use your testing and research to give the architect a really clear brief on your vision and your target audience to help them with the designs.

Planning permission

This, along with business rates (which you'll read about later), is the most fundamentally frustrating process I have ever gone through in my life. I am not a planning expert, so the advice I give below is based on my own personal experience and learning curve, and I would highly recommend you seek the services of an expert in rural planning (rural planning consultant) to find out what the regulations are before embarking on a farm diversification project, especially if you are living in a greenbelt area like I am. A greenbelt area is a 'specially designated area of countryside protected from most forms of development. It is protected to help stop urban sprawl, preserve the character of existing settlements and encourage development within existing built-up areas.'[7]

Every planning authority or council is different, so the key learning points I introduce around planning permission will depend on how proactive your local planning authority is towards farm diversification. Within this book I am referring to the English Planning System and this may differ for Wales, Scotland or Northern Ireland.

1. You need to be clear from the outset that if you change your premises from residential use to business use it will be extremely difficult to change them back in the future. For redundant barns you are often required to prove that there is no potential business use before you can apply for residential status. The reason for saying this is to make sure you take the decision to apply for planning permission to convert your building very seriously.

2. You need to be prepared for how long it takes to get planning permission, as well as the costs involved. Planning applications take considerable time to prepare due to the amount of information

---

[7] www.planningportal.co.uk

required (see later in the chapter for further details on this) and also the need to discuss matters with the local authority, as authorities vary. Your local authority will hopefully be more supportive than mine was. My application was originally rejected and it took around eight months (and that was with a considerable amount of pushing) for the application to finally be approved. I was warned that if I rushed this process there may be consequences, and it is advisable to get the groundwork right before submitting your application. The reason for this is that when you submit the application, the planning authority of your local council may ask you for further information before the application is validated. For this reason I would highly recommend seeking the services of a rural planning consultant to help you.

3. Every planning authority is different when it comes to planning permission, and I recommend you submit a pre-planning application before you start. Most councils offer a pre-application advice service, which can save you time and money before you put in your application, helping to identify key planning issues and

requirements which can minimise delays and costs. I submitted an initial pre-planning application to a local Planning Officer which was completely rejected on 7 December 2010. Working with my planning consultant, I had to endure hours and hours of work to win the planning permission battle and my application was finally submitted on 13 May 2011 – five months of hard work later.

4. If you are going to use a planning consultant, my advice is to make sure you get an up-front cost for the planning support – my consultant ended up putting in over 80 hours of work to get the application up to submission standard. Later in this chapter I give an overview of all the different reports I had to produce in order to obtain the planning permission.

5. I was able to access some free support through the Rural Planning Facilitation Service (RPFS). This service is operated across the North West of England and provided a free planning audit for proposals to promote and assist farm diversification and rural development. I would urge you to make enquiries as to whether there is a similar service in your area by contacting local business support services.

To obtain planning permission, these are all the things you may need to either obtain or think about. Before going to the expense of obtaining this information, do check with your local planning authority as to what information they require as this varies by council. It is difficult to give you cost estimates as they will vary and be dependent on a number of factors, including the size of the property, the number of buildings, the location, the intended use etc. But do not underestimate the amount of time and cost involved in assembling all the above information. I spent around £10,000 in total; this included application fees and the costs of producing the reports.

Required action	Details
Seek pre-planning application advice	Costs vary by planning authority and this can take around two months to obtain.
Complete the planning application form	You will need to pay a planning fee of around £350. Costs vary by planning authority and the size of the area – the bigger the area, the higher the fee.

Obtain technical CAD drawings (note that architectural drawings are not required for a planning application)	You can get free software to create these drawings and if you search for 'CAD drawings' a variety of different software packages will come up. My planning authority asked for the following drawings: <ul><li>Location plan (at a metric scale of 1:1250 or 1:2500) showing the site edged in red, with the rest of the holding edged in blue</li><li>Existing and proposed floor plans (at a metric scale of 1:50 or 1:100)</li><li>Existing and proposed elevations (at a metric scale of 1:50 or 1:100)</li><li>Existing and proposed roof plan (at a metric scale of 1:50 or 1:100)</li><li>Existing and proposed site plan (at a metric scale of 1:200 or 1:500).</li></ul>

Structural survey of the premises. As we were planning to use an old barn as a wedding venue, we were asked to pay for a full structural survey report	The building inspectors wanted proof of the suitability of the barn for public use and that the barn met current British Standards for loadings. The survey is needed to assess the current structural condition of the building you wish to convert (especially if the building is a former agricultural building) and to make recommendations on any essential structural repairs considered necessary as part of conversion and general refurbishment works. I searched for 'agricultural building surveyor'.
Topographical survey or a scaled land survey	This shows the area of interest and all natural (e.g. trees, large rocks) and man-made features (e.g. buildings) with contour lines.

Design and access and planning policy statement	This included coordination with architects, planners etc., online application forms and full submission of the planning application. My design and access and planning policy statement was written by my planning consultant and was 29 pages or 16,000 words in length.
Bat and owl survey	Otherwise known as a protected species report, this is at the discretion of the local authority but I was required to produce one.
Archaeological building survey or heritage statement	This is at the discretion of the local authority and can sometimes be a condition of planning permission.
Landscaping scheme	The planning authority may wish to see how you intend to deal with landscaping – especially if a car park is required and you live in a greenbelt area.

Full traffic impact assessment	I had to use a transport consultant to prepare a Green Transport Plan. The document details how you will seek to minimise the impacts of travel by reducing the need for journeys, reducing the number of single-occupancy car journeys made and by encouraging the use of sustainable modes of travel, such as walking, cycling, public transport and car sharing. Do not underestimate the impact of transport. You need to consider the impact that bringing 100+ people with their cars into a rural area will have. Your neighbours may not be happy and may start to complain. Transport must be one of the top areas which you take time to consider.

Noise. When you open, especially if you are converting an existing building, make sure you address the implications of noise in advance as this issue may turn around to bite you, especially if you have neighbours	We ended up having to completely seal the roof to prevent sound escaping. The basic rule is that if air can escape so can sound, so you do need to think about insulation and sealing the existing roof (if it's a barn conversion) to the best of your ability. From the outset, I contacted a noise monitoring company and produced a report to address this issue. I was always against a 'cut-off power monitor' as I felt this would ruin the business (couples are advised NOT to book a venue which automatically cuts off the music if it gets too loud). The line we take around music is to maintain good communication with the Bride and Groom and our method of noise control rule is that if the bar staff can't hear the customer ordering drinks at the bar when the music is 25 metres away, then it is too loud.

Recommended strategies

1. Take lots of photos of your plot from particular vantage points across the area from where you can see your farm/plot. These will then be used to determine which areas of your land can be viewed from the wider area, so that the visual impact of any car parking can be assessed. The aim is to show that the car parking area won't be visible from any of the surrounding public roads or vistas.

2. Enclose your business plan with your application, including a market analysis and evidence from local suppliers as to the benefits of the venue. It is also helpful to map out potential local employment opportunities which your development could provide (particularly for young people).

3. Look for similar applications/businesses which have been granted planning permission in your area or nearby. Go to your local planning office and look through all the supporting information that was submitted in support of another successful planning application, as this is what the planning authority will be looking for.

4. Influential contacts. It's helpful if you can get to know and seek support for your development from your local councillors, your local MP, your Chamber of Commerce, Tourist Information

Office, neighbours, council neighbourhood manager for your area etc. The council is required to consult neighbours and a number of statutory consultees as part of the planning application process. However, it's a good idea for you to encourage your local councillors and anyone else who is happy to support the application to write to the planning authority when the 21-day consultation starts.

5. If your proposed development is based around the conversion of a farm building, then you are likely to be in a greenbelt area. Within greenbelt areas there are a whole load of regulations around siting, scale, materials, design and landscaping, and ensuring that the build, traffic and activity generated by the proposals will not unacceptably affect the amenity or character of the area or harm people's enjoyment of the countryside.

6. Finally, remember that – often before commencing any building works – you may need to discharge planning conditions. So, rather than rejecting a planning application, a planning authority might grant permission, but with attached planning conditions. Some conditions may require approval by the planning authority before development commences (such as agreeing the colour of

materials), while others can be discharged during the course of development (for example, limits to site operating hours). I had to provide samples and obtain approval in writing by the Planning Officer of all external walling, roofing and fenestration materials I was going to use.

After we submitted all these reports, the Planning Officer came back with a list of amendments and queries as well as a request for an extension to the eight weeks in order to allow time to deal with the amendments. I did find this process incredibly frustrating as I couldn't seem to get across to the Planning Officer the strategic advantages of the application. I asked for someone higher up in the Council Planning Department to look at the application as I felt I had wasted enough time and effort with the local Planning Officer. I then pressed for the application to be heard at the Council's Highways and Planning Committee on 18 August 2011. This was a gamble as the application could have been rejected. The application was presented at the committee meeting and planning permission was secured – eight months after the original application had been submitted.

I wanted to give you as much information as possible on planning permission and the process so that you are forewarned that the process is costly, time-consuming and extremely frustrating. I wish someone had warned me at the outset that I would need all this information. My background in fighting a judicial review (through gathering evidence and writing reports) and doing an MBA (from gaining insights into developing strategies and handling failure) gave me the fighting spirit and resilience I needed to get through it.

Over to you…

- Reflect on the lessons above and learn from my mistakes.
- Seek advice from a rural planning consultant early on.
- Make sure you seek to address noise and transport considerations with local neighbours from the outset – not addressing these crucial issues could potentially mean planning permission rejection.
- Be prepared for the cost and the time it will take, and remember that you will need to be patient and resilient.

Designing and implementing your construction project

It's not just an architect and plans you will need…

You've finally got your planning permission and during the process you will have found your builder. Below is a list of some other things I wish I had known about construction and transforming a building. Many of these actions should be undertaken by the architect and the builder working together as a team to oversee the construction. To save money, I unfortunately did not do any of this as I should have – as you'll find out later.

Required action	Details
Before you appoint your builder, you should really have everything finalised, in particular elevation drawings and Building Regulations/structural approval.	When you have your plans, you will need to find the right contractor (builder or person overseeing the construction process) and this will usually mean that you will need to have – at the very least – a basic specification to send to builders to accompany the planning drawings. This is so that you can obtain some indicative quotes from a number of builders (I went for the best of three) in order to give you an idea of the potential costs of your proposed development. I used the website www. MyBuilder.com to obtain the building quotes.

Your architect may want to meet with a structural engineer to discuss the structural requirements of your build, e.g. steel structures and joist specifications.	This will then need to be calculated by the engineer to ensure sizes are suitable for the commercial loadings which will be applied – especially if your proposed build or change is above ground floor level.
The architect will normally work alongside a mechanical and electrical (M&E) specialist/consultant who can recommend what systems to use according to the proposed day-to-day usage of the building.	The architect will then provide full drawings and specifications for all your requirements so that you can provide the building inspector with the required information, including full specifications and drawings for heating, ventilation and electrical installations. They will also be able to advise on utilities and possible solutions for if you aren't on mains gas on water, for example, such as renewable energy sources. The consultant can also put together a tender package for you to send out to specialist contractors so that you will have competitive tenders and hopefully a better price for the work involved.

There are numerous consultants who can meet with you to discuss in further detail the usage patterns and requirements for the property so that they can best design an appropriate system for your needs.	You will hear terms like SBEM (Simplified Building Energy Model), SAP (Standard Assessment Procedure) and EPC (Energy Performance Certificate) calculations. These are all government-approved methods for measuring energy use and the environmental performance of buildings and are needed to demonstrate conformity to Building Regulations.
Fire Regulations. I would definitely urge you to develop good relations with your local fire department. Make sure they visit as early as possible so that you can explain your plans and find out what they may be looking for.	We had a great fire officer who came out and explained all the fire precaution measures we would need to think about. As we lined the barn with timber and used parachute linings to hide the corrugated metal roof, we had to treat these with a Class 0 fire retardant spray as well as obtain fire certificates for other furnishings we were going to use.

Over to you...

- Recruiting a good architect is crucial; they will be able to help you find the right builder by providing you with the right plans and drawings to obtain accurate building costs.
- The architect will also help you with appointing other consultants and engineers – this is essential and can save you money, time and frustration.
- Make sure the builder you appoint has experience of commercial projects.
- It is really important that you develop good relations and involve the fire department from the very beginning.

Building inspectors

You will need Building Regulations approval from your local building inspector. Planning approval means you receive permission from the local authority to build your new venture. Building Regulations approval is a completely separate process and ensures that the proposed building or structure is going to be built in full compliance with Building Regulations.

An important part of getting approval is having a building inspector carry out regular site visits to ensure that you are adhering to and are compliant with the many regulations. You can either use a local authority or an independent building inspector; you will need to submit your plans for Building Regulations to them in advance of starting your build. It will pay to get the building inspector on your side – reach out to them for advice while still at the planning design stage to ensure that what you are proposing will be compliant. Your architect should be able to help with this.

I ended up using independent building inspectors as they allowed the builders to start on site almost immediately after the drawings were completed, allowing some time for the builder to order materials and mobilise his workforce. I was told that local authority inspectors would probably want a couple of weeks to mull over the drawings before even making any comments, which was time I just didn't have.

During the build, I left it to the builder to liaise directly with the building inspectors. They wanted to carry out checks at key stages of the build. They wanted to see the floor and ceiling joists and thermal and sound insulation we used. They came up to inspect the depth and proximity of drains and manholes and to inspect the foundations. They were also very interested in the fire safety precautions we put in place.

Managing the build

You've found your builder and your architect and you have your building inspector appointed. Here are the lessons

I learned about managing the construction project. If I had known what I know now, I would never have agreed to oversee the construction myself and would have paid for the project to be managed by an expert such as the architect.

Required action	Details
The Construction (Design and Management) Regulations 2015 require that a CDM coordinator is appointed on projects that last for more than 30 days or involve more than 500 person-days of construction work.	The CDM coordinator's role is to advise the client on matters relating to health and safety during the design process and during the planning phases of construction. When a CDM coordinator is appointed, they will want to see that the contractor has in place a Construction Phase Health and Safety Plan. Not having this document puts you at risk in the event of an incident on site. When you start a project as big as a new venue, the Health and Safety Executive will have been informed about your project and could visit the site to inspect your paperwork without any warning. In theory, your builder or contractors shouldn't be on site without this document.

The contractor will usually sort out plumbers and electricians. Make sure they have commercial experience and knowledge so that they are up to date with the latest regulations – especially electricians – for things like emergency lighting, fire regulations etc.	My biggest tip is to make friends with these two categories of contractors as you will need them again and again in the future. Once you've found a good plumber and electrician, cling onto them for dear life!
Good plans and Building Regulations approval mean that you will have a much clearer idea of the building costs of the project and will manage the risk of overspending. I faced a huge learning curve in managing the build, as although I had obtained a quote from the builder, I kept asking the builder to do extra things. 'Can you just do this…' became my favourite saying!	You must ask the builder regularly for a statement of expenditure against the quote and monitoring of any extra costs that have been incurred. Make sure you do this from the outset – don't wait to face a problem like I experienced.

The renewables maze. I used several government-funded bodies to help advise me about renewables. They can also help you to find any potential grant funding available.

At the time, I used an organisation called Envirolink Northwest. They help businesses in the North West with support on installing renewable and low-carbon technologies. Their assistance was free, impartial and professional, and at any stage of your project they can help you with the following: choosing the right type of energy generation system (e.g. solar panels, wind turbines, ground source heat pump, biomass generator) that best suits your business needs; identifying when planning permission is required and how to go about obtaining it; how to connect to the electricity grid; options for financing your project; how to benefit from the government's finance incentives for generating electricity and heat from renewable sources.

Having explored all types of renewables, due to our location and being 800 ft above sea level, the wind turbine was the best energy generation option. However, you do need to undergo a difficult planning application process for this, and again a range of supporting reports will be required.

You must look from the outset into water supplies, electricity, fat traps and sewerage and future proof your development. If you don't consider these now then you could face problems in the future.	For example, although we are on a mains water supply, the one water pipe feeds four other farms and in the height of summer when you are facing up to 15 weddings a month, your water supply and especially your water pressure may be stretched. We have now had to install our own dedicated water supply for the farm at considerable cost. Similarly, we had to install a new three-phase electricity supply when we developed the site and think about a backup generator. Finally, we had to install a water treatment plant and hugely expand our fat traps. Make sure when you are doing this that the plant you select and install is large enough to cope with any future expansion plans.
Make sure you think about signage from the outset as this will need to be included in your planning application, otherwise you may be forced to submit a separate planning application as I had to do.	I found it incredibly difficult to obtain brown tourist signs for our venue and it really pays to make some good contacts within the local council.

Fixtures and fittings

I was running out of funding and very concerned about how I would be able to equip my facility – especially the cookery school. I came across the brochure of a national kitchen equipment provider whose brochure focused on 'wellbeing in your environment', had recently launched a range of energy-efficient appliances. These appliances would complement the mode of cookery school I was developing – being powered by a wind turbine and having no gas on site, I needed to source the most energy-efficient equipment available!

I ended up making a phone call to a national company asking if they would be interested in sponsorship. The area Sales Director (Philip) asked me to email him back to explain what I was developing.

I provided a brief overview of the facility and then wrote to him. 'I know you have a cookery school based in Woking, Surrey but as far as I can ascertain, don't have any cookery school presence in the North. I was therefore wondering whether your company would be interested in an association with The Wellbeing Farm. If you would be able to supply the ovens, induction hobs and extractor fans at a reduced rate, we would then ensure that your products are promoted throughout the venue and on our publicity material. I would be grateful if you could pass this email onto the relevant person within your organisation and if you would like to come and see the premises, we would be more than happy to facilitate a visit.'

On the back of a phone call, I received sponsorship for the entire cookery school, so the moral of the story is be brave and don't be afraid to pick up the phone!

Most of the furniture and furnishings used around the farm were sourced from eBay and more recently Facebook Marketplace (which didn't exist when I first set up the farm). I could write another book just about the experiences I had with picking up items I'd purchased via eBay. For example, I bought my original café chairs from a McDonald's car park in Birmingham. I obtained my first bar from an Indian restaurant in Altrincham, and my second bar from a former nightclub in Manchester. I bought a sink from a stately home in Scotland. The parachutes lining the ceiling of the wedding barn were ex-military parachutes used for landing a small tank or jeep.

Figure 3.1: My brother Harry transforming the barn

Over to you...

- Think about how you could creatively furnish your venue – obviously this depends on your target market, but Pinterest is a great resource for ideas.
- Think outside the box, be creative and source ideas from other venues – this is why visiting other establishments is so useful.
- Speak to your local business support unit for advice on any grant funding that might be available to you.
- Be brave and don't be afraid to pick up the phone!

Telephones, computing and Wi-Fi

Research how many phone lines can go into your farm, as you may be physically restricted. Phone up BT Openreach or a similar company to get some advice on this. Remember, you'll need a few, especially if you'll be using credit card machines.

You don't need a server. At the beginning I had the huge cost of installing one but eventually moved my entire business over to cloud-based systems and now the server is redundant. When thinking about your IT and phone systems you'll need to consider the following:

- Actual telephones – are these going to be internal or wireless and what voicemail systems will you need?
- How many phone lines will you require?
- What Wi-Fi service will you need? You will probably need two types – one you can use to access your systems via laptops, PCs etc. and another for guest use that will be restricted to browsing capability.
- What IT systems will you use? We use Google Drive, Dropbox, Event Temple, Xero – all cloud-based systems.
- Good IT and phone support and maintenance are essential when running a busy venue. You'll need to make sure this includes all parts, labour and software. How quick are the response times and will you have 24/7 availability?

Animals

In case you are wondering, when did the llamas arrive? The llamas were one of the earliest arrivals at the farm as I had to get them early to have time to train them. Being inquisitive in nature, they enjoyed watching the comings and goings of the construction workers building the farm. Although I had purposely purchased quality llamas who had been trained from birth for trekking, they obviously didn't know our farm or local area. To prepare the llamas for meeting the public, they had to be walked several times a week in order to prepare them for every scenario so they wouldn't go crazy when faced with a member of the public. I'll never forget the time I was walking the llamas along Plantation Road when a farmer did an emergency stop with his tractor right alongside us. He leaned out of the window and said, *'I've been farming in these parts for 30 years and I've never seen anything like that!'*

Figure 3.2: The llamas outside our family business,
Whitehead's Butchers

Business rates

I hadn't even opened for trading when the Business Rates Inspector called.

First of all, be very wary of companies who approach you out of the blue claiming they can reduce your business rates. I was cold-called by one of these companies, whom I won't name, who said they had reviewed my business rates and told me that they could significantly reduce them. Unfortunately, as we were a new business and they promised a significant reduction to my business rates, I signed a contract for them to do the work on my behalf and to lodge an appeal with the Valuation Office. To cut a long story short, I received an invoice from the business rates company for nearly £1,000, claiming they had done a lot of work on formulating, surveying and completing negotiations for the business rates appeal for my property. However, I subsequently found out that they had never actually re-surveyed the property and I contacted Trading Standards about my case. It transpired that the firm who had contacted me to reduce my business rates were an unlicensed firm of surveyors.

Prior to diversifying we paid approximately £2,000 in business rates, but once we had diversified the Valuation Office wanted circa £17,000. Not expecting this huge increase in business rates, I starting doing a lot of work to find evidence of my business being over-assessed. I've got to admit that I spent a considerable amount of time during the trading year of 2013/14 fighting the business rates decision I had been given. Receiving a court summons for failing to pay business rates in your first year of trading is an extremely upsetting experience, particularly after you've taken the time and effort to write at length explaining your circumstances.

My findings and personal observation were that the Localism Act resulted in what can only be described as a postcode lottery when it comes to business rates assessment. Councils in areas with a large farming population seem to favour farm diversification and be understanding about the difficulties of setting up a new business in a rural area. They seem to charge lower business rates etc. than councils in areas with more urban populations who are not as considerate and who do not understand the challenges of setting up a business in a rural area.

Although business rates are charged based on the size of your establishment, what the Valuation Office fails to recognise is the problems rural businesses face when perhaps only 20% of their buildings are being used – particularly when starting a new business. Also, having funded the cost of a diversification, as a new business you face hefty repayment fees in terms of bank loans etc. and therefore won't make any profit. Making a new business pay £17,000 in business rates when the business is growing and initially running at a loss seems wrong.

It seemed wrong that the Valuation Office was comparing the farm against businesses which were established 20 years ago, who offer accommodation and have approximately 250 acres of land, when I am a diversified hill farm with no accommodation and with just 30 acres on a minor road. Surely they should be comparing like for like when it comes to business rates assessments?

I set about this massive challenge, which took weeks and weeks to sort out. First of all, I had to prepare a list of all the businesses they'd compared me against and one day I actually got in the car and drove 126 miles to every single one of these 15 businesses. I got out of the car and I took photographs of each building and where they were located. When I got back, I Googled each business, obtained their financial reports and pulled together a compendium of evidence to demonstrate the absurdity of the assessment.

I gathered my huge compendium of evidence and on 27 November 2014 my appeal was heard by a tribunal sitting in Manchester. I found the experience totally overwhelming. I actually got the National Farmers Union to come and support me and they wrote the whole case up as a case study for farmers, because of the craziness of what had happened and why I was facing all this. I did win the case and they revalued my rates, which went down considerably, so the exercise was worth doing, but to be quite honest it's yet another example of when you think you've got a really good idea, you're trying to create employment opportunities, you're trying to change a run-down farm into something that will help the community and all you get is block, block, block.

Here is my advice to farmers and others concerned about business rates valuations:

1. Before you think about diversifying, get an assessment done of the likely effect of diversifying on your business rates and think whether you could set your new business up as potential subsidiary companies.

2. Be wary of making your farm diversification buildings too extravagant – stick to basic materials, keep it as rustic as possible and even avoid central heating if you can!

3. Challenge the valuation methodology – it was unfair that this was calculated solely on the price per unit area basis. There were a number of inaccuracies within the assessment, primarily based upon the Valuation Office including buildings like the farmhouse which we lived in (which we were paying Council Tax on) or buildings that should have been agriculturally exempt.

4. Take care to read how the Valuation Office classifies you and don't just accept the valuation you've been given. Look at comparable valuations for other similar businesses around the country and fight your case. Put a proposal to the council that you will pay £xxx per month until your business rates are reviewed. They can't serve a

court summons if you are making a proposal to pay something towards the business rates.

5. Do your research –look thoroughly into the businesses you've been compared against – is your rating fair? I'd recommend physically going to visit the places you've been valued against and take photographs to submit as evidence. I drove over 100 miles in a day doing this and shared my photographic evidence with the tribunal.

6. Submit an application to the council for business rate relief and hardship relief – councils do have discretionary powers to offer hardship relief to struggling firms.

7. Get support from your MP, your Ward Councillor and the Cabinet Councillor who looks after non-domestic rates.

8. If you do get to a tribunal, they will want to see a common-sense approach – think along the lines of 'Would anyone be prepared to pay £xxx for this building? What would you rent it for? What would you expect to pay?' You need to convince the tribunal that you are acting in a fair and reasonable way. Argue that your business can't afford rates of £xxx per year.

9. Be very wary of commercial firms approaching you and saying they can help get your business rates down – they will force you to sign contracts and then you will have a battle with them as they will demand large amounts of money for doing hardly anything.

Over to you...

All you can do as a land-owner is challenge what has been done, do your research, gather together your evidence, and go and appeal to the common sense of the Valuation Office.

I hope that this chapter hasn't put you off designing and overseeing the transformation of your premises. As I mentioned at the beginning, everything in this chapter I found out about the hard way – from making mistakes. If someone had given me a comprehensive guide to all the things I needed to think about, the process would have been so much easier. I therefore hope you've found this comprehensive chapter helpful and an eye-opener to all the things you need to think about when creating your venue from scratch.

The transformation of Wheatsheaf Hill Farm

Figure 3.3: Wheatsheaf Hill Farm before transformation

Figure 3.4: Wheatsheaf Hill Farm after transformation (Photo
credit: Weddings Vintage Photography)

Figure 3.5: The old sheep shed before transformation

Figure 3.6: The old hay store (which is now the Wedding Barn)

Figure 3.7: The old stable block during transformation
(which was transformed into the Cookery School)

Figure 3.8: The barn before transformation

Figure 3.9: The Wellbeing Farm (Photo credit: EJS Aerial)

PART TWO

Running your business – experimenting, managing the team and the money

Chapter 4

It's a numbers game – the importance of cash flow

The best entrepreneurs are not the best visionaries. The greatest entrepreneurs are incredible salespeople. They know how to tell an amazing story that will convince talent and investors to join in on the journey.

Alejandro Cremades, *The Art of Startup Fundraising* (2016)

I remember applying to colleges when I was 16. I was sitting in on a conversation between my dad and my tutor when the tutor turned to my dad and said, 'There is no way Celia will pass her maths O-level.' I think that comment planted something in me. A reaction to 'how dare you say I'm going to fail at something – I'm going to prove you wrong.' I obtained a C grade in my maths O-level – OK, not an amazing grade, but I did pass.

When it comes to running a business, everything comes at a price and knowing your numbers is huge – in fact, as a business owner it is THE most important thing you need to master. I learned this the hard way.

The numbers lessons I have learned

Securing funding

If you don't have the money to start your business, then it's not really going to get off the ground.

A great source of funding is grant funding. I was lucky to receive grant funding from my local council and from the Rural Development Programme for England (RDPE), which helped hugely to fund the capital costs of building the farm. The RDPE provide money for projects to improve agriculture, the environment and rural life. The only drawback to securing grant funding is the amount of paperwork you have to do and the time it takes to complete the application. For example, although I was successful in securing the RDPE grant funding, I had to attend a workshop which was mandatory as part of the grant funding. In addition, as part of the conditions of the grant I had to meet certain milestones around project and building delivery and submit grant claims according to their specified timescales. Each quarter I had to submit invoices and bank statements and claim expenses back in arrears. Failure to keep to their timescales could mean that you lose your right to claim that element of eligible costs.

When I had the idea of developing my own business in 2011, all the many innovative ways to raise finance, such as crowdfunding, angel investors, Funding Circle etc. didn't exist. The only options for raising finance were personal savings, friends, family, grant funding or a bank loan.

Whatever your source of funding, you will need to be prepared to give potential funding providers a coherent business plan, that is, the business context into which you are planning to launch your company.

You will need to include:

- What your business will do
- Who your customers will be
- Why people will visit your venue (or need your products/services)
- Evidence that a market exists and its potential
- Evidence of why your business will survive when others don't
- Analysis of the competition
- Who you are and why you're going into business
- Why you believe you've got the skills and expertise (qualifications and experience)
- How you will fund the setting up of the business
- How you will repay any money you borrow
- What your ongoing costs and overheads will be (in the form of a cash flow statement)
- Sales and revenue forecasts for the first 12 months of business
- Details of suppliers and contracts
- Your goals for the first 12 months and beyond, and your critical success measures in relation to the proposed venture.

Along with your business plan, they may want to see at least six months' worth of bank statements to assess your financial position.

When I worked in the NHS we created business plans, but these were huge, lengthy, complicated documents with masses of evidence. So when it came to creating the business plan for my business with the aim of using this to secure bank funding, my first version was over 50 pages long. Armed with this impressive wad of paper, I started contacting banks on my own. I met with several bank funding managers and just kept getting rejected. I was rejected by five banks in all.

Eventually I discovered an organisation called Access to Finance (www.a2fnw.co.uk) who took my 50-page document and slimmed it down to around five pages. With a streamlined, more focused business plan and a more robust and accurate cash flow forecast, I went back to the bank and the funding was secured. A year ago (June 2018) I discovered Gino Wickman and his Traction methodology[8] who has a great two-page model of a business plan.

---

[8] G. Wickman, *Traction: Get a Grip on Your Business* (2011).

Over to you...

- A good business plan can be written in just two pages. Don't over complicate things – keep it simple. So often our experience of working in large bureaucratic organisations like the NHS makes us unprepared for becoming an entrepreneur.
- The moral of this story is to keep it simple – 'less is more'.

Managing your money

When your bank loan comes to fruition and the money is in your bank account, life gets easier. You can start to afford things, the building starts, you can hire staff and things start to happen. However, if you've not planned how you will use the money you have in the right way – if you don't budget and manage your money – it will soon disappear.

In the early days, when I first opened the only way I could survive was to use credit cards – luckily in my previous role as an NHS Director in a secure, stable job with a good pension, I had a good credit rating. A good credit rating which resulted in many offers of credit from credit card companies – gold dust to a struggling first-time business owner. The credit card people still thought I was a director in the NHS so I could still get all this money, and all this time these letters kept coming through, zero percent interest for 18 months. Fantastic, you think. Another one comes through and you accept it, so I was effectively running the business on credit card loans. I used to manage everything on credit cards, constantly juggling from one 0% finance offer to another.

I remember looking at my bank account and I never knew how much money would be in there. Some days would be pleasant and some days you'd feel sick with worry, thinking, 'How am I going to pay the bills – let's get the credit card out again.' It's like when you go to a cashpoint to withdraw money and the screen reads 'insufficient funds in your account'.

I could never get my head around VAT – I didn't really deal with VAT in the NHS and I didn't really cover it during my MBA, so I really struggled to understand it. So when I received this huge demand for money every quarter, known as the VAT bill, it always came as a surprise. I started using my credit cards to pay my VAT bill. One day, I rang up the VAT office with my credit card to pay my VAT bill and the officer said, 'We will not accept a credit card. You've paid on so many credit cards before and we won't accept it.' For me this was one of the worst moments in my life. It was December 2014 – which as a hospitality venue should be your peak time –

and I was struggling to pay an £8,000 VAT bill. I felt sick
– I had employed staff who were relying on me, suppliers
demanding me to pay their bills, bookings which we had
to deliver on. I was in trouble, facing a mountain of debt
and I just didn't know what to do. Something had to
change.

I couldn't bring myself to tell Stephen or anyone else
what a mess I was in. It was an 'ostrich head in the sand'
moment. The only thing I could do was to write letters
to my mum and Stephen. I just couldn't bring myself to
actually speak to them without getting very, very upset.
Until you are facing potential bankruptcy, you will never
know stress quite like this.

So, I wrote this letter and laid out how much debt
I was in. I wrote, I do have a plan to resolve this but I
need some more money. I had to describe my plans to
get myself out of debt, but it meant spending. I needed
another £10,000 on top of the £8,000 to pay the VAT bill,
but this plan would solve my problems. Now, from their
perspective, I'd already borrowed, borrowed, borrowed.
I'd been lent money, family money. I'd spent my family's
money and then there I was asking for more money. I'd
promised them this business was going to work but now
here I was – failing – asking for more money. I will always
be eternally grateful to my mum for trusting me and for
lending me the money to pay that VAT bill and for the
things I needed to do to transform my business into a
wedding venue.

Figure 4.1: The transformation of the barn into a wedding venue

Over to you...

- Are you using credit cards to fund a business or lifestyle you can't really afford?
- What resources and savings have you put aside to cope for unexpected situations?
- Have you got a dedicated bank account for your VAT and tax?

Having faced potential bankruptcy, I put in place systems to ensure that this never happened again. These systems are described below.

Changing your accountant and insisting on robust, accurate and regular financial information

- Insist on regular financial information from your bookkeeper or accountant. You need a simple monthly finance report to give you some information on financial monitoring for members of the company to discuss at monthly meetings. My accountant now joins us at monthly meetings, fulfilling a Finance Director-style role in the business. A good accountant should be the right-hand person of the business.

- To run your business well, you need to know your break-even point (the revenue necessary to cover your company's total amount of fixed and variable expenses during a specified period of time) and have a basic cash flow management system in place with budgeting.

- I have VAT inspection insurance provided via my accountant to prepare me for any VAT inspections which could lead to large accountancy bills if you are not covered by insurance.

- I have gone through five accountants to find the perfect one – don't be afraid to change your accountant if they are not giving you the support and information you need.

- My current accountant visits my premises once a month and produces a graphical cash flow forecast created using Xero, with indicators which clearly show where my shortfalls are going to be, where I'm going to have low months and what I'm going to do about it – it's all projected forward. I now have around eight sheets of paper given to me in report format every month, with graphs showing the value of weddings booked to date, what weddings I've got booked for the following years and so on, as well as a profile of the income that has been invoiced, how much has been paid out and what's due for payment. I have a really clear picture of what's happening on the financial side of my business. I then have graphs showing me my cash balance and where it's going and how it's moving – great accounting information with all the jargon and confusion stripped away – exactly what a business owner needs to run a business effectively.

Using a good accountancy system

Be organised with your receipts, bank and credit card statements. Find a bookkeeping/accountancy system that is easy to use and preferably cloud-based, such as Xero or Quickbooks, so you can log in from anywhere.

Having multiple bank accounts

I read the book *Profit First* by Mike Michalowicz[9] and although I haven't implemented the full Profit First system, I did take on board his suggestion of having a number of different bank accounts. This has now become one of the most essential things that has helped me to manage my finances and cash flow.

I have six bank accounts:

1. Day-to-day expenses. All the income comes into this bank account, and from this I transfer money into other accounts.
2. Profit account. I put money aside to fund investment and to fund future weddings.
3. VAT account. I make sure I always have enough money in this account to pay my VAT bill — it is important that this account is never touched.
4. Income tax. This is money I put aside to pay my income tax bill and pay off my bank loan.
5. Emergency. I always make sure I have money set aside to cover any emergencies or cancellations.

---

[9] M. Michalowicz, *Profit First: Transform Your Business from a Cash-Eating Monster to a Money-Making Machine* (2017).

6. Staff Experience Fund – this was a new concept for 2019. For every wedding I put £xxx into a Staff Experience Fund. This funds team-building days and rewards for the staff.

> **Over to you…**
> There is a minimal charge for extra accounts, but the transformational effect it has on running your business and helping you with cash flow is amazing – I would definitely recommend speaking to your bank about opening additional accounts.

Budgeting
I've got to be honest, I'm not really very good at this, but my accountant has set me indicative budgets around each area of my business. These are very detailed and after three years of robust, accurate accounting these budgets are accurate, so I do try to stick to them. Your accountant should be able to advise you and help you to create a budget for your business.

Having procedures and policies for everything
In June 2018 I read *Traction: Get a Grip on Your Business* by Gino Wickman,[10] which has to be the one book that has

---

[10] Wickman, *Traction*.

made the most fundamental difference to my business, so much so that I made the whole team read the book and get behind the implementation of the Traction concept. This has led to considerable changes in the business in terms of productivity, drive and implementation.

We now have documented over 200 processes covering every area – 'How To' manuals are now in situ, providing me (the business owner) with the reassurance that the business is being run effectively. This has meant that I can now focus solely on the growth of the business – and on writing this book. As part of the Traction process, the team also worked together to produce a weekly scoreboard – which they produce for me every Wednesday and which shows us the marketing and sales activities that have been undertaken and how near (or far) we are to reaching our business goals.

> **Over to you...**
> You need to start documenting how you do things in your business. Creating a set of 'How To' manuals for your business is a really good idea, so that in case of holidays or sickness, someone knows what to do.

Pricing
I used to price my products by obtaining wedding brochures from other businesses and basically copying their prices. How wrong was that approach! Every

business is different and you can't accurately cost out your business this way. Again, my accountant Martin helped me to cost and work out the prices I needed to be charging by gathering information on the costs of production, staffing, overheads and other things to work out an accurate pricing model. This is the task you also need to do.

Over to you...

- Ask your accountant for help with your pricing model and how to go about calculating accurate prices to provide you with the right level of income to not only break even, but to make a decent profit too.
- Stick to your prices and let some clients go elsewhere if you don't fit into their budget.
- Don't be afraid of failure. I support failing because if I hadn't failed at this business, if I hadn't failed at paying the VAT bill, if I hadn't failed at so many other things, I never would have learned. I don't think I would have transformed the business and it wouldn't have grown as much as it has done now. I almost embrace failure because you can only get better by things not going so well in the first place.

The numbers have played a big part in getting me to the place that I'm at today, because I've now got clarity and, in many ways, looking back, the phone call from the lady at the VAT office did me a big favour. If she hadn't refused to accept my credit card, I would probably have carried on as before and I wouldn't have changed. I also learned the hard way the difference between an inferior and a fantastic accountant/bookkeeper.

Chapter 5

Business processes and systems – how to ensure your venture will be a success

Many small businesses are doomed from day one, not from competition or the economy, but from the ignorance of their owners… their destiny is already decided because they have no idea how a business should be operated.

William Manchee

It was only when I read Gino Wickman's book *Traction*[11] in June 2018 that I came to appreciate the importance of systems and processes in a business.

At that time, we had brainstormed everything we do to run The Wellbeing Farm and produced pages and pages of things we needed to think about. At the time of writing this chapter, we have documented over 200 processes covering every area of the business. Going

---

[11] Wickman, *Traction*.

through the huge process of documenting everything we do has allowed me to begin to relax and work *on* my business rather than *in* it, because everyone involved now understands and follows the processes we have established. This huge operating manual covers what we do to deliver events, including running the business, managing payments, how we sell a wedding, how our marketing systems work, all our health and safety processes, our recipes and so on. Systematising my business in this way has provided the business with clarity, productivity, a sense of ownership by the staff and freedom for me, the business owner.

So what are the important systems and processes you need to think about when running a busy venue or business?

We streamlined the entire Wellbeing Farm business into six groups of activity, each with a handy acronym (Figures 5.1–5.6).

Figure 5.1: The ALARM Staff Support System

Figure 5.2: The SMILE Sales and Marketing System

Figure 5.3: The SHAPE Wedding Planning System

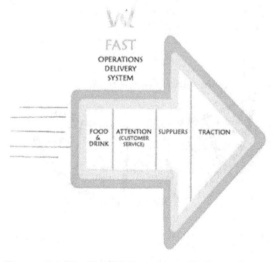

Figure 5.4: The FAST Operations Delivery System

5.5: The SITE Premises Plan

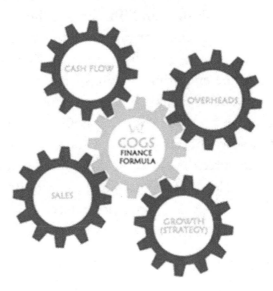

5.6: The COGS Finance Formula

Applying the principles of Gino Wickman's *Traction*[12] meant we had to improve the structure of our team meetings and run them to secure engagement and progress with projects within the team.

Gino Wickman calls these weekly Traction meetings 'Level 10 meetings'. These are important to ensure that our time in the business is spent on the most important things around the business and to ensure that progression of the business is at hand.

- Our Level 10 meetings are held at 2pm EVERY Wednesday promptly. (We work from Wednesday to Wednesday at present.)
- We start the meeting with a discussion of 'Any good news you wish to share?' This breaks the ice for the staff and helps them engage with the meeting.
- We then move onto discussing the **Scorecard** to monitor the enquiries, bookings, viewings, meetings and provisional bookings the company has received within the previous seven days, all of which helps us to know whether we are on track/behind against each measure. The scorecard is produced by the team and provides weekly performance monitoring on marketing, sales and conversion rates.

---

[12] Wickman, *Traction*.

- We then move on to the **Rock Report** (again a term used in *Traction*); this is an essential list of projects/ processes that are required to be completed during a 90-day period (depending on the size of the task). We simply mark these as **green** or **red**, which indicates whether the task has been completed or not – there is no in between. (Once the rocks for the period have been completed, a meeting with the business owner is scheduled for the new tasks for the next period to be inserted on the rock report and circulated to the staff.)

- We then move on to the **Customer/Employee Headlines** – we ask the question 'Are the customers/ staff happy and what, if any, problems do we need to solve?'

- The next part of the meeting is the **To Do List**, a seven-day list of action items which need to be completed before the next meeting. We check whether we are on track with the previous week's actions. What has been completed and what is outstanding?

- The final discussion we have is **IDS (Identify issues, Discuss them, Solve them)** – again another term used in *Traction*. This gives the team the opportunity to discuss any concerns which may have arisen during the last seven days and enables us all to work together to agree on a solution to resolve them.

The weekly Level 10 Traction meetings focus the whole team on performance and delivering quarterly (90-day) projects. The business owner (Managing Director) works with the team to identify projects that will deliver improvements to the business – these are either projects to improve internal systems to ensure the smooth running of the business, or projects which improve the experience for customers and their guests.

Over the next few chapters I go into more detail around the essential systems and processes you may need to develop.

The ALARM Staff Support System

ALARM = **A**dvertise and Recruitment; **L**earning and Training, **A**chievement and Advancement; **R**eward; **M**orale and Motivation

Staff engagement and morale play a huge and very important role in the success, drive and growth of the business. Employee engagement improves productivity and performance, which in turn creates additional revenue and profit. While writing this book I was lucky enough to receive a copy of *Recruit, Inspire & Retain: How to Create a Company Culture to Grow Your Business* by Jacqui Mann[13] which I will be following (like I did Gino Wickman's *Traction*) and implementing the relevant

---

[13] J. Mann, *Recruit, Inspire & Retain: How to Create a Company Culture to Grow Your Business* (2018).

systems and procedures. More details on the importance of managing staff are given in Chapter 7.

The SMILE Sales and Marketing System

SMILE = **S**ocial Media; **M**aterials (brochures, printed materials etc.); **I**n-person (wedding open days, wedding fairs etc); **L**ikeability (Know, like and trust – blogs, this book etc.); **E**vent Temple (Sales monitoring, emails – Event Temple is the customer relationship management system we use).

Sales and marketing form a huge part of my workload, and it is right that the business owner focuses much of their attention on this area as it is the lifeblood of the business. Further information on sales and marketing can be found in Chapter 6.

SHAPE Wedding Planning System

SHAPE = **S**upport; **H**elp; **A**dvice; **P**rops; **E**xperience

Two books helped me to develop our customer services model and we used these to form the SHAPE Wedding Planning Support System. The books were *Difference* by Bernadette Jiwa[14] and Donald Miller's book *Building a Story Brand*.[15]

---

[14] B. Jiwa, *Difference: The One-Page Method for Reimagining Your Business and Reinventing Your Marketing* (2014).

[15] D. Miller, *Building a Story Brand* (2017).

Both books helped me to really understand what our couples wanted from a wedding venue and helped us to connect with our customers, thus supporting the growth of our business. *Building a Story Brand* uses a framework to help you work out what your customer wants from your business and what problems they face (or their perceived need for your business); you then empathise with them and develop a plan to help them. More details can be found on Donald Miller's website (www.storybrand.com/how-to-tell-a-story).

Bernadette Jiwa's book, *Difference*, provides you with another great framework to use – The Difference Map (www.difference.is) and allows you to identify an idea, examine your customer's problems and desires and finally help them – it is really good at teaching empathy.

Mapping the Story Brand and The Difference Map can create very powerful marketing messages for your business.

FAST Operations Delivery System

FAST = **F**ood and Drink; **A**ttention (customer service); **S**uppliers; **T**raction ('the way we do things round here')

All our chef's recipes are documented in the form of a Chef's Operating Bible, so in the event of a chef not turning up, our relief or agency chef can take over because all the recipes and the way the food is served and presented is documented through a series of photos in the operating bible; this ensures consistency of food and service provision.

I always wanted the food and drink we served to be different from the norm. I set about researching wine, looking for animal themes and quirky labels (which was a huge challenge to our wine suppliers). This ensured that, where possible, our food and drink offer stood out and was memorable.

To deliver the weddings and to ensure a consistent level of customer service, for about the first 50 weddings my role was to sit and observe. I would be at the wedding with a clipboard, paper and pen noting down everything that was good or bad about the wedding. After every wedding, I would feed back my findings to the team and where necessary we'd come up with ways to improve our offer, documenting everything into a before, during and after the wedding process. After a while my feedback on improvements got less and less and I knew the process we had was working. I'm pleased to say that since doing this work, I've actually not been physically present at a wedding for a while (apart from obviously popping in to say congratulations to the couple and to check that the staff are OK). This is how you as a business owner get freedom – by putting in the work and effort to create the systems and processes to run your business.

On a final but very topical point, in 2011 when I started work on creating The Wellbeing Farm, I wanted to ensure that we were doing our bit to save the environment. Therefore, where possible we have used renewable technologies – we are powered by a wind turbine, we use energy-efficient materials, we source local suppliers and we recycle as much as possible. We have won several awards for our green business work, including being awarded a Gold level in the Green Tourism Scheme (www.green-tourism.com). We were proud that while most businesses in the scheme progress from Bronze to Silver to Gold, the scheme owners held a special meeting to discuss our application as it was so unusual for a new business to enter straight in at Gold level. This decision, to focus on being a green business from the outset, has really paid off especially given the importance many customers now place on sustainability.

SITE Premises Plan

SITE = **S**afety (Health and Safety); **IT** (technology, computing, phones etc.); **T**ransformation (outside and interior improvements; **E**nhance/Fix (DIY/short-term repairs)

In Chapter 3 I discussed the premises at length and described how the business has been transformed from a collection of neglected farm buildings into an award-winning venue and all the things I needed to consider at the time. However, when you open your doors, you'll find that improvements to the premises never end. Having a venue in the middle of a farm means we continually need to keep abreast of regulations and health and safety concerns.

My background of working in the NHS has made me very risk-adverse when it comes to health and safety. Knowing that the three main problems which could close a business down are finance, staff, and health and safety, I have ensured that we have robust systems and processes in place in these areas. I researched to find one of the best companies in the UK to manage my staff policies and processes and health and safety systems and have 24/7 advisory cover. I have a comprehensive set of risk assessments in place with a cloud-based system, which notifies the team and myself when health and safety processes need reviewing or action is required.

The following tips are a list of the things you need to consider when it comes to health and safety.

- **Tip No. 1 – Fire.** I've already explained in Chapter 3 the importance of establishing good relationships with the local fire brigade and seeking their advice in the design stages of your build. Similarly, when you are ready to open, seek their help and support in undertaking a fire risk assessment. Don't skimp on this important step as it is essential for running a business. All staff will need regular fire training and you will need to test your emergency lighting and fire alarms on a regular basis. Fire extinguishers need servicing every year. We also get our equipment PAT tested on a yearly basis (a PAT test is a routine inspection of some types of electrical appliances to check that they are safe to use). We are strict about ensuring that no candles, fireworks, sparklers, cigarettes or lighters of any kind are brought into the barn. Nor may e-cigarettes be used in the barn; we provide a smoking area outside the premises.

- **Tip No. 2 – Licensing.** You will need to get your premises approved for marriages and civil partnerships if you want people to be able to get legally married at your premises. Your local authority licensing department will be able to help with this, although be aware that it is a lengthy process, so don't leave it until the last minute to sort this out. Similarly, another licence you will need is an alcohol licence (unless you are just going to provide the venue and not any alcohol). I have paid for six members of staff to have a personal licence (a personal licence is required by anyone authorising the sale of alcohol from a Licensed Premises. All Licensed Premises must have an allocated Personal Licence Holder, known as the Designated Premises Supervisor (DPS). The DPS must authorise every alcohol sale.

Both the alcohol licence and the approval of premises licence involve putting announcements in local papers and some form of public consultation, so be aware of the time this all takes. To help with my approval of premises licence application, I used the services of an ex-policeman who was great in sorting out everything I would need to put in place. Once you receive your alcohol licence, you will need to ensure that staff are trained and that appropriate systems are in place to check the ages of people purchasing drinks to negate the risk of under-age drinking. If you employ young people (aged 18 or under), measures must be put in place to protect them under child protection legislation.

- **Tip No 3 – Food hygiene.** We produce and prepare all the food for our events on-site. You may want to start out by hiring/using caterers. Whatever you do, you will need to ensure that robust food hygiene systems and policies are in place. The Food Standards Agency (www.food.gov.uk) offers guidance on the types of flooring and work surfaces which are deemed acceptable. You need to think carefully about the slip resistance of flooring such as tiles, particularly if these could get wet. Floors need to be sound and have smooth, impervious, non-absorbent and washable surfaces. The Health and Safety Executive website contains further information on this (www.hse.gov. uk). I used the services of an environmental health officer (EHO) to put everything in place for me. Unfortunately, EHOs now charge around £60 per hour for non-statutory services. The Industry Guide to Good Hygiene Practice[16] gives advice on ensuring compliance with the legal requirements and also provides information on good practice.

Finally, staff need to be trained; I ensure that all my managers and the Head Chef are trained to a Level 3 food hygiene standard. Paperwork is extremely important and daily temperature and monitoring checks are critical. I devised a system of undertaking monthly spot checks, like an EHO would, to ensure that food hygiene and allergy monitoring is continually up to the necessary standards.

A hugely topical issue at the moment is that of allergies – there have been cases recently where restaurant owners have been jailed for manslaughter after serving food containing nuts which had been certified as nut-free to allergy sufferers. Venues really need to be on top of the issue of allergies and everyone has a role to play in making sure you adhere to best practice. We make sure that couples complete forms and sign off on allergy and dietary requirements in advance.

- **Tip No. 4 – Insurance.** Insurance is critical and I have made sure that I'm covered for almost every eventuality. I receive a lot of support from the Federation of Small Businesses who provide a great

---

[16] Department of Health, *Industry Guide to Good Hygiene Practice: Catering Guide* (2018).

helpline on insurance, HR and legal issues, covering all sorts of risks a small business can face.

- **Tip No. 5 – Security.** Unfortunately, if you are a licensed venue, guests will try and smuggle alcohol in. We've learned and taught our staff about the tricks people use. Our farm also has a good CCTV system and electric gates for additional security outside of trading hours.
- **Tip No. 6 – Business continuity.** I thought I was prepared for every eventuality until an electricity failure at a wedding caused me to revisit my business continuity plans. I spent the first three months of 2019 completely reviewing all of our health and safety processes and procedures, and sought the advice and services of a specialist business continuity company, who helped me to derive a business continuity plan of action. This is now in place and includes a brand new generator!
- **Tip No. 7 – Data protection and recovery.** With the ever-looming danger of cybersecurity facing businesses, ensuring that your business is fully protected and has systems in place for data recovery is essential. This includes password control, safe storage of data, ensuring compliance with the General Data Protection Regulations (GDPR) and making regular backups of your data.
- **Tip No. 8 – Pest control.** How much of an issue this is will depend on your type of premises. We are based on a farm with animals, which presents its own challenges. At some stage you will likely encounter some type of

vermin, so I have always seen pest control as essential. We have a service which is maintained by a third-party contractor. They come out and monitor bait boxes, check for activity and replenish poison if needed.

- **Tip No. 9 – Waste disposal.** Don't underestimate the amount of waste your venue will generate. I have hardly any landfill waste (due to our green business practices), but do generate masses of recycling. I use a food waste collection service to collect leftover food, which is then turned into fertiliser. You will need to notify your local authority about the waste disposal practices you have in place. You don't have to use council services and I'd shop around for the best deals.

- **Tip No. 10 – Cleaning.** My motto for the staff is 'If you are leaning, you should be cleaning.' Due to my background in the NHS, I am quite fastidious about cleaning and have ensured that pre- and post-event cleaning checks are in place for every area. Third-party cleaners are issued with detailed checklists to comply with cleaning standards.

- **Tip No. 11 – Animal care.** I've included all the animals' vaccination records, vet checks, dentistry, foot care and cleaning into my automated risk register so I get reminders when something is due. The animal handlers also have pre- and post-event checks and cleaning checklists to complete.

- **Tip No. 12 – Maintenance.** Again, I use an online risk assessment system to remind me when equipment/

maintenance servicing is due and also to remind the team weekly, monthly and quarterly about other maintenance tasks. For example, every year we schedule power-washing of the animal buildings in preparation for the wedding season. In hindsight, when I set up the business, I should have documented every piece of equipment when I purchased it (i.e. created an asset register), noted the care and maintenance instructions and scheduled these in. That's a good tip if you are setting up your business from scratch.

- **Tip No. 13 – Weather.** Luckily, in the six years we've been trading we have only had one year with really heavy snow. That year the weather was so bad I put in place a robust adverse weather plan and processes. I even purchased an ex-local authority snowplough attachment for our tractor!

COGS Finance Formula

COGS = Cash flow; **O**verheads; **G**rowth (strategy); **S**ales

I explained many of my finance checks in Chapter 4. I learned the importance of numbers and cash flow the hard way and the processes and monthly monitoring which I now have in place enable me to sleep at night.

We constantly monitor our overheads and every month we pick a different overhead on which to focus on and try to reduce costs or improve supply by renegotiating with suppliers.

Our company focuses on 90-day working (from Gino Wickman's *Traction*) to enable the business to constantly grow and innovate, and our close monitoring of sales means that we continue to experience growth even in these uncertain times as the country negotiates its way through the Brexit process.

I remain convinced that having robust systems and processes in place is the key to business owner and entrepreneurial freedom, and I believe these principles can be applied to any business, not just those in the hospitality sector.

Over to you…

- The principles around putting systems in place and documenting procedures can be applied to anyone and any business.
- If I were to start building my business from scratch again, I would have started documenting these processes much earlier and revising them as I learned lessons and improved.
- Documenting your systems and processes leads to freedom for the business owner and true sustainable business growth.

Chapter 6

Finding, marketing and selling to customers

....

The media wants overnight successes (so they have someone to tear down). Ignore them. Ignore the early adopter critics who never have enough to play with. Ignore your investors who want proven tactics and predictable instant results. Listen instead to your real customers, to your vision, and make something for the long haul. Because that's how long it's going to take.

Seth Godin

....

How you connect with and market to your customers is critical, and the most important role a Managing Director/CEO of a business can fulfil is to focus on sales and marketing, because bringing in new business is the lifeblood of any business.

Start by ensuring that you have clearly identified your ideal, archetypal customer. When you know who they are, you can start to target your marketing and sales efforts and design a brand that speaks directly to them – this will make sales so much easier. For example, our ideal customer for The Wellbeing Farm fits the following profile:

- Age: 26–42
- Location: Within a 30-mile radius of the farm (Manchester, Liverpool, Preston, Lancaster, West Yorkshire, Clitheroe, Bolton, Bury, Stockport). We are lucky to be very centrally located in the North West.
- Interests: Sustainability, food and drink, DIY weddings, creativity, animal welfare, yoga
- Characteristics: Time poor, requiring a venue which will do everything for them
- Financial position: Professionals, doctors, dentists, teachers, bankers
- Our customers are very much concerned about their guests having an amazing experience. They want to have a fun, relaxed, laid-back wedding with good food. Ideally they would love a personalised wedding but being professionals, they may have little time to organise everything themselves.

There are some marketing and sales approaches I've tried which have been really successful and others less so. Let me give you a brief overview of the techniques that have worked for me and why.

The wedding industry is all about making connections with your ideal customers (the couples who will be booking your venue), so your marketing and sales techniques need to focus around building your know, like and trust factor – building credibility and getting people to know and understand your brand and trust that you will do a good job in delivering their dream wedding.

Having a sales system

A sales system is absolutely essential for a wedding venue, and our conversion rate hugely increased when this was put in place. To create the sales system, the team and I thrashed out everything we did onto a series of flip charts and Post-it Notes. We then created an email campaign to support the system, together with touch points. The first system I used was Infusionsoft (www.Keap.com). This worked well but the back-end system was very complicated and required me to hire an Infusionsoft specialist every time I needed to change anything.

We revised our sales system after I read Gino Wickman's book *Traction*. Our target audience is millennials, who appreciate a variety of communication channels according to what we need to tell them. We therefore needed a system which could not only cope with phone calls, texting, video messaging, emails and face-to-face communication, but would also help us plan and design the wedding and also enable online signatures for the various agreements the couple would need to sign. We developed a specification and set about shortlisting various customer relationship management (CRM) systems for the farm. At the time (2018), there was one which particularly stood out from the others – Event Temple (www.eventtemple.com). Since summer 2018, we have used this system to automatise our entire sales process, which gives me as the business owner visibility in terms of enquiries, bookings and conversion rates. Each week, the information from Event Temple is put onto a scoreboard and performance is discussed at team meetings.

Techniques to build credibility

Testimonials

We have found gathering testimonials to be a really great way of building credibility. We make a point of asking couples to hand-write a few words about their wedding in a large, plain notepad. I find that a hand-written testimonial feels considerably more genuine and credible than a typed one, and because it's hand-written and hopefully accompanied by a photo of the couple (we use an Instax camera to obtain a photo of the couple), it then provides something which you can share on social media and on your website.

Feedback

Since I started the business I created a feedback system on hand-written cards based on the Net Promoter Score. According to their website, the Net Promoter Score 'measures customer experience and predicts business growth. This proven metric transformed the business world and now provides the core measurement for customer experience management programs the world round.'[17] I'm pleased to say that we have baskets and baskets of hand-written feedback forms which validate the excellent service standards we provide with further credibility.

Consistency

For a couple of years now we have been opening every Wednesday between 5pm and 7pm for 'Wedding Wednesday' and although at first this was difficult to build up, we find that having that Wednesday evening 'no appointment necessary' slot is really helpful for couples who are working or find it difficult to visit during the day or at weekends.

Wedding open days

We have held monthly wedding open days since we began, although it is only within the past two years that we have started theming the open days. Every January we hold several open days throughout the month, as for a wedding venue typically 40% of bookings for the year come in the month of January due to Christmas and New Year

---

[17] www.netpromoter.com/know

engagements. We don't use many third-party suppliers at our open days as we prefer to use the opportunity to showcase our venue and all the props which couples can use to decorate the room. Wedding open days are a great way for couples to come and see your venue and for you to sit down with them and give them a quote for their wedding.

Quirky Wedding Fair

We hold two wedding fairs each year in March and October which we have branded as 'The Quirky Wedding Fair'. I became very disillusioned with wedding fairs, as very often I found them to be bland, boring events with no atmosphere where couples would walk around a multitude of very ordinary white-tableclothed stalls. I wanted our wedding fair to be different and I toured the country visiting the best wedding fairs in the UK to gather ideas. We make sure our Quirky Wedding Fair is fun, engaging, informative and helpful, and we hand-pick suppliers who are compatible with our brand – fun, unique and magical. The Quirky Wedding Fair is not an opportunity to generate bookings and conversion; it's more of an opportunity for suppliers to showcase their services and for couples to book with them. Nevertheless, it's a good way of supporting suppliers and their marketing.

Awareness days

Emma Etheridge from the Wedding Biz Club (www. weddingbizclub.com) provides a fantastic monthly resource of awareness days (which are typically set up by charities and other organisations to raise awareness of a particular cause) and how you can use these in your marketing. We try and link our social media engagement to awareness days as far as possible.

Social media

Social media has been essential for my business. Facebook, Instagram and Pinterest work particularly well. I spend a lot of time on Facebook, finding quirky and educational stories to share with couples to incorporate a fun element into wedding planning. Similarly, I'm proud that our Instagram and Pinterest pages are focused on ensuring that the content is visually engaging. We maintain a presence on Twitter and LinkedIn, but we don't use them as much as the other platforms for wedding marketing. I find Google My Business essential and we are actively building up our Google following. As our target audience is millennials, a lot of our engagement with couples is also through Facebook Messenger using ManyChat (www.manychat.com).

Facebook group

We set up a private Facebook group for couples who had booked their wedding at the farm to keep them engaged and to feel special by having a private group. This works particularly well as a platform for couples who have booked the venue to share ideas and experiences, to keep them informed and to communicate our developments. Being a private group means we can control the membership, meaning that the content is very relevant to them.

Facebook Live and Instagram Stories

I enjoy recording Facebook Live streams, particularly at events like wedding open days to showcase the venue. I've not embraced Instagram Stories as much as I should have, and these two areas will be a big focus to drive visibility throughout 2019.

Gifts

We provide a really lovely pack when couples book our venue – a WOW Pack. We've taken time to source and develop small gifts which don't cost much to post. We have created and give couples access to a secret wedding planning website full of downloadable checklists, planning advice and videos to help them with their wedding planning (based on what I learned when I trained to be a professional wedding planner). We found personalised wedding countdown plaques to be a great gift for couples, together with 'I'm getting married at The Wellbeing Farm' keyrings.

Physical brochure

A high-quality physical brochure is, I believe, an essential element for wedding venue marketing. We post all our brochures out in a nice pack rather than sending them by email. It's so easy to press delete on an email, but if you receive a nice brochure in the post, we reckon it's harder to throw away – or the couple may give it to someone else if they aren't interested in what we have to offer.

Video messaging

We use BombBomb (www.bombbomb.com) or video messaging to create personalised video messages for couples which are then emailed out. This has been a really useful tool for engaging with prospective couples and for conveying difficult or complex information.

Text messaging

Millennials love their phones, so we use mobile-friendly communication channels to contact the couples, such as having a mobile-optimised website and using text messaging and Facebook Messenger, which we find is a particularly good way of reaching out to our target audience.

Use the telephone

We still find incoming and outgoing phone calls to be one of the most effective ways to engage with people. We've learned that couples seem to prefer to take phone calls during the evening (that's why Wedding Wednesday is a great help). We use a phone answering service to ensure that we don't miss any calls, and one of my principles is that phone calls need to be answered within three rings. We have also found Facetime to be a great tool in selling weddings and have booked several weddings for couples from abroad using this tool.

Using images

Our wedding coordinators are told to take pictures of the weddings and to liaise with the wedding photographer to write up a summary of each one into a short social media post. Images are one of the most important tools you can use to sell your venue, particularly for weddings where everything is visually appealing. Having sought permission from the couple, we work with our supplier photographers and videographers in advance to encourage them to share their images of the wedding for us to use in our marketing, obviously acknowledging the photographers and videographers at the same time. We also use the images in photobooks which we have available for couples to flick through when visiting the venue and on photo posters which we have on display at wedding open days.

Video

Having a video of our venue was a real game changer. In September 2016, I used a local videographer to help me create a video based around a wedding and narrated by the bride, Daniella. There was no pre-written script, but I was careful to pick a bride who would come across very well, who would be likeable and was confident. Who better to pick than a wedding singer who had chosen The Wellbeing Farm as her wedding venue over hundreds of other wedding venues at which she had sung? What further endorsement do you need? Following the introduction of the video, our conversion rate quadrupled. Nearly every bride who watches the video bursts into tears as it resonates so well with them and captures the emotion of their ideal wedding.

We call our weddings 'Weddings with the WOW factor', as the minute a couple enters the barn doors, 'WOW' is often the first word to come out of their mouths. I think the video perfectly portrays why our weddings have that factor and the results of the video have been amazing.

The video works because it tells a story:

- It explains how the couple found the venue and the urgency to visit and book.
- It appeals to my ideal customer.
- It showcases every aspect of a wedding and clearly outlines the benefits of having a wedding at the farm.
- It gives potential customers an overview of exactly what weddings at The Wellbeing Farm are all about

and, at the same time, seeks to address any potential concerns they may have.

- The food plays a major role in the video because that is what we've built our reputation on – particularly with our family business, Whitehead's Butchers.
- It is full of glowing testimonials from guests and even the bride's father!
- It shows entertainment, fun, magic, quirkiness, alcohol and great food – key essential elements for a great wedding.
- It comes across as very genuine whilst not being too salesy...
- It has a clear call to action at the end.

I am delighted to say that the video won The Best Business Video award at the 2016 National Entrepreneur Awards and we still use it as a key selling tool for our weddings.

Website

I am now on my fifth website since starting The Wellbeing Farm, and moved over to a WordPress platform in 2018. The website works really well and the design was developed by studying some of the most successful website designs and obtaining design suggestions from the team at the Entrepreneurs Circle. The website links through to Event Temple (www.eventtemple.com) and we also use an online appointment booking system called YouCanBookMe (https://youcanbook.me) which has been another game changer in getting couples to visit our venue. I have a part-time web designer who maintains my website and keeps my Search Engine Optimisation (SEO) up to date.

Photoshoots

In the early days when you are first starting out, staging fake weddings for photos and images and holding photoshoots is a great way to showcase your venue. In fact, when I first started out, a member of my team, James, had to step in to act as the groom for the photos!

Blogging and vlogging

These are great for increasing your venue's authenticity, credibility and the 'know, like and trust' factor with your target audience.

Third-party websites

I use these to promote awareness of the venue and find the best ones (at the time of writing) to be Bridebook (www.bridebook.co.uk), the Natural Wedding Company (www.thenaturalweddingcompany.co.uk), For Better For Worse (www.forbetterforworse.co.uk) and Eventbrite (www.eventbrite.co.uk). I did find, however, that the website that charged me in excess of £1,000 for listing the venue didn't attract the right types of couples for my venue, so you've got to be careful where you spend your money on these and use your Google analytics to make sure that the third-party websites you choose do actually target your ideal couples and help increase the profile of your venue. Incidentally I have never tried Google advertising.

Awards

These have been a great tool for growing my business and I am proud to have recently won the North West Wedding Venue of the Year (Countryside) at the National Wedding Industry Awards. My proudest moment, however, was winning Lancashire Wedding Venue of the Year in 2016 at the Marketing Lancashire awards. I was so excited that I paid for my whole team to attend the awards ceremony. For me it represented the recognition that we had finally made it in the wedding industry. I found that the sooner you can have the confidence to start entering for awards the better. My top tip is to begin the application form with a paragraph demonstrating the attributes they are looking for so that they have concrete evidence of your achievements.

Radio

I have found local radio shows, particularly BBC Radio Lancashire and BBC Radio Manchester, to be really helpful for increasing the profile of the venue. I have been interviewed on the radio several times and they have also done live radio shows from the farm. Getting the involvement of local radio stations really does help to support and promote new businesses.

Local press

Our local paper, *The Bolton News*, has been incredibly helpful in generating free publicity for the farm, and I make a point of keeping them informed about any key developments. Maintaining good relationships with your local media is essential to any business, and improving my public relations skills is a key area I want to focus on in 2019.

Other marketing techniques that have helped grow my business include:

Networking

I did this all the time when I first set up my business, and many of the business connections I made in the early days are still in contact with me today. Networking is essential to grow relationships and contacts, particularly with suppliers and key influencers. These days I don't do as much networking as I used to and if I attend a networking event, it has to be at a really unique venue which I've always wanted to visit. I'm a huge advocate of just being brave and making connections. I remember convincing Blackburn with Darwen Council that the venue would be a great choice for the Mayor of Blackburn with Darwen to include in his civic tour on 18 September 2013. I also emailed StartUp Britain to see if the national StartUp Britain Bus would visit the farm to promote rural businesses – and yes, the bus did make a visit to the farm on Tuesday 30 July 2013. We even got one of our llamas to board the bus!

Newsletters

We use MailChimp® (www.mailchimp.com) to send out a monthly e-newsletter with updates on our events, new props and any key developments on the farm, and to assist with the engagement of couples who have not yet booked with us. We try to keep the wording succinct, use great images and make the newsletter informative, including details of future events, new farm developments and helpful advice for couples.

Filming opportunities

We are very lucky to have the BBC based in MediaCityUK, Salford – just 20 miles from the farm – and we have been featured on a couple of television programmes, including North West Tonight. My dream would be for the farm to appear on Countryfile and I live in hope!

Reviews

You can't really be in hospitality without a presence on TripAdvisor (www.tripadvisor.com). It's a great search engine and a good platform for sharing photos and obtaining reviews. Similarly, people use reviews on Facebook and Google to give you feedback. There are clear, unwritten rules to using TripAdvisor and other review sites effectively. It's important that you keep your customers in mind at all times and stay true to their needs. Avoid simply trying to 'game' the system; this isn't ethical and you may get caught out. Here are my top five recommendations:

- Always acknowledge the review, whether good or bad.
- Try to see the point the reviewer is making and put yourself in their shoes – whatever you do, don't get defensive.

- Keep your response short, sweet and simple and try to empathise with the reviewer.
- Keep monitoring the reviews and look out for any negative reviews which people prefer to use this platform for.
- Don't get upset by negative reviews and complaints. I used to get really upset if people left an adverse review or complained – I'd end up taking it really personally or the judgemental side of me would appear. These days I don't take things to heart as much. It's not that I don't care, but I see adverse reviews and complaints as signs that we haven't got everything perfect yet and use them as an opportunity for improvement. I know it sounds like a cliché, but you've really got to embrace and love failure. When you are failing, it's awful at the time and you think, 'How on earth will I ever get over this?' But you will. Not only will you get over it, but you'll be stronger. You'll be more determined to succeed. Just make sure you realise that owning and growing a business never follows a linear, straight line of growth. It's going to be up and down like a rollercoaster, so just be prepared to enjoy the ride of your life.

So, I hope I have given you some food for thought and ideas on how you can promote your venue and raise your credibility and visibility to your customers.

Over to you...

- As a business owner, sales and marketing is the lifeblood of your business.
- Take time to identify your ideal customer, as you can then begin to target your marketing and sales efforts and design a brand that speaks directly to them.
- Once you've identified your target customer, try a variety of different approaches to market to them – from social media to physical products.
- Be inventive, test ideas and try to be different from your competitors in what you do to sell and market your services.

Chapter 7

Wise up – overcoming staff issues and barriers and becoming resilient

You don't build a business. You build people, and people build the business.

Zig Ziglar

When it comes to managing staff, I've got to confess I don't like it. It's my area of weakness. I would far rather be generating strategies, developing new ways of marketing etc. than managing the day-to-day issues which arise with staff management. For that reason, the greatest success I have had is to recruit managers with really good people management skills who can fulfil that role for me.

The year 2015 represented a huge turning point for the farm, with the realisation that I had to do a lot more to develop a culture for the business. This began later that year, so 2015 was branded internally as 'the year we became awesome'.

After trading for around 18 months, I reached a business and personal crisis on 1 December 2014. I was running out of money, had experienced a run of difficult staffing issues and the business was in a mess. I wrote a paper to pen down my thoughts, called 'What Happened to The Wellbeing Farm'. I had done a lot of reflection and tried and tested a lot of things, ways of working and our offer to customers. Our reflection was defined in a series of papers called 'Reflect, Review and Celebrate'.

I had to try to explain to a young team that the business was failing and that we needed to do something radical to save it. I gave the team examples of how the best people in the world, like Thomas Edison, Abraham Lincoln, Steven Spielberg, Richard Branson, Colonel Sanders, Sylvester Stallone and James Dyson, had initially been rejected or faced failure. I taught them about the road to disappointment we had been on and we discussed a concept called Blue Ocean Strategy (www.blueoceanstrategy.com) based on a book by W. Chan Kim and Renée Mauborgne[18] and how we needed to change the business to differentiate ourselves from competitors and create The Wellbeing Farm 'Best in Class Express'.

---

[18] W. Chan Kim and R. Mauborgne, *Blue Ocean Strategy: How to Create Uncontested Market Space and Make the Competition Irrelevant* (2005).

We started work on company values 'the way we do things round here' and I remember reading the story of Innocent Drinks. A specific paragraph in particular reached out to me and I read it to the team:

> *When we're all old and grey and sitting in our rocking chairs, we want to be able to look back and be really proud of the business we all helped to create. We think the best way of achieving this is by living the values that are closest to our hearts. Our values need to reflect what we are, how we do things, and where we increasingly want to be.*[19]

I told the team that we needed one word which would underpin everything we would deliver and what we wanted our customers to say after they had visited The Wellbeing Farm; for example:

- The Wellbeing Farm is a _____ place to work
- My experience was _____
- The food was _____
- The service was _____
- The attitude of the staff was _____
- The wedding/party was _____

---

[19] Innocent Drinks, *A Book about Innocent: Our Story and Some Things We've Learned* (2009).

The word we chose was 'awesome', inspired by the 'The Awesomeness Manifesto' of Umair Haque,[20] who explains the four pillars of awesomeness:

1. Ethical production
2. Insanely great stuff – delight, inspire and enlighten
3. Value
4. Staff love working there.

Haque goes on to describe that 'awesomeness happens when value is created by people who love what they do, added to insanely great stuff and multiplied by communities who are delighted and inspired because they are authentically better off'. I decided that this was to be the ethos of The Wellbeing Farm.

We were going to deliver awesome experiences which involved satisfying customers' requirements, giving great customer service and constantly exceeding customer expectations. So the start of 2015 was all about refocusing the business on the areas we knew would work. The key element was that everything would be pre-booked and nobody could come to the farm without prior arrangements. This meant I could manage staff rotas, costs and service demand in advance.

---

[20] U. Haque, 'The Awesomeness Manifesto', *Harvard Business Review* (16 September 2009).

So The Wellbeing Farm was changed to deliver:

- Awesome corporate events
- Awesome functions (funeral wakes, parties, hen parties, baby showers etc.)
- Awesome rustic farm weddings
- Awesome afternoon teas
- Awesome llama trekking experiences (only llama treks with afternoon tea – we no longer just do llama treks)
- Awesome cookery courses
- Awesome large-scale events (Open Farm Sunday, Harvest Festival, Christmas Fair)
- Awesome quality food – running a cookery school as part of the farm's offering allowed us to show our customers just how serious we are about food.

We decided to no longer provide school visits, children's parties, craft and wellbeing courses or a petting farm. All the animals (except for the llamas, donkeys, sheep and chickens) were sold. We had spread ourselves far too thinly – we couldn't market the farm to both schools and corporates at the same time – and our offer was confusing to customers.

We developed a manifesto for the farm which goes as follows:

- We are clear about our goals and we aren't afraid to make them happen.

- We have an 'AWESOME' philosophy which we aren't afraid to live by, and we have 'blue ocean strategies' for how we deliver our products to customers.
- We are focused and determined to deliver on daily, weekly, monthly, quarterly and yearly goals.
- We deliver awesomeness into every area of our business.
- The Managing Director works *on* the business, not *in* the business. (At the time I was the person cooking the meals, serving in the café and so on. I was too focused on the day-to-day running of the business instead of growing it.)

Great brands stand for something – they are clear on what their promise is. So you need to ask yourself, 'What is your brand promise? What does your brand care about and what can it deliver?' Make sure you take into account what your target customers actually want and what the competition are not offering. Your brand values should be simple, motivating, distinctive and true. You then need to make sure your product or service delivers against them. Your product or service must actually fulfil the brand's promise.

Innocent Drinks say, 'for success, as a business we should pass "the granny test"... you should be able to explain your business idea and how it will beat the competition in a simple sentence that your granny would understand' (this is sometimes known as the elevator pitch). You should also have a sense of purpose. The granny test and sense of purpose for The Wellbeing Farm became: 'We deliver awesome experiences. We provide a venue where we deliver awesome experiences – these experiences are not only fun, but also give you the opportunity to de-stress, relax and enjoy our peaceful atmosphere and to also support British farming.'

Staff were given customer service training on how to answer the phone, how to take a booking and how to deliver an event or experience. For example, the phone had to be answered promptly (within three rings). We wanted people to experience a sense of 'fun' and to experience wellbeing and de-stress when they visited the farm. We deliver memorable experiences for people, and we made it our mission to go above and beyond for our clients and customers and to wow them. Our aim was for people to leave saying, 'That was an awesome experience…' and we used the Net Promoter Score to actively monitor how customers felt about us.

One of the principles Gino Wickman emphasises in his book *Traction*[21] is the need for you to develop core values which everyone develops and operates by and which create your culture. So, in the summer 2018, our new culture – the 5 Ps – was developed by the staff themselves through questionnaires and a staff event. Staff were invited to complete anonymous questionnaires,

---

[21] Wickman, *Traction*.

choosing from a selection of 30 values which ones they felt were important to the farm. These were condensed down to a handful of values during a staff event to galvanise and strengthen team morale.

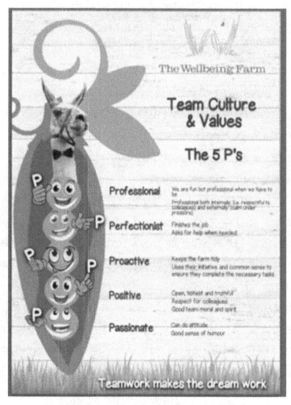

Figure 7.1: Our poster showing the 5 Ps

More recently, having attended an Entrepreneurs Circle event at which Nigel Botterill (www.nigelbotterill.com) summed up his company culture, we have adopted a new way of working focusing on three principles which are fun and resonate with the team:

- Do great work – try to always work to the best of your abilities.
- Don't be an arsehole – be a team player.
- Give a shit – care about the business and what you are doing.

Our poster depicting our team culture and these three values can be seen in Figure 7.2.

Figure 7.2: Our poster showing the culture of Team Wellbeing

I'm not going to turn this section into a human resources handbook – there are plenty of books around which will describe the process of staff management in far better ways than I can. However, in six years of managing staff, I've learned a few things which I will now explain in a series of tips to help you with your staff management, too.

Tip No. 1

I have engaged the services of a top HR firm to develop and manage my human resources processes and to provide me with 24/7 HR protection so I can sleep at night. After six years of running my business, I feel I have faced every staff issue around and realise the importance for the business owner of having quality HR support. I feel that as the staff know that I have appointed the services of a top HR company they feel valued and appreciated.

Tip No. 2

Nowadays I let the team recruit their own members (zero-hours staff only) based on the values of the business. We obviously have job descriptions, person specifications and a documented recruitment process, but we advertise roles locally (mainly using Facebook) and I get members of the team at all levels actively involved in the recruitment process.

Tip No. 3

For full-time positions, we have adopted the Entrepreneurs Circle's X-Factor recruitment methodology,[22] which provides a really robust style of recruitment, and some of our best candidates have been recruited using this approach.

Tip No. 4

We give the staff opportunities for growth – I used to find it so frustrating when I was younger and nobody would hire me because I didn't have the right experience. Young people are enthusiastic, have great skills, haven't been tainted by working in other businesses and are keen to learn. When I recruit staff I always find out about their talents and am keen to fully utilise these. I currently use a 17-year-old part-time waitress to help me with my IT. Another waitress turned out to be a fantastic graphic designer and another turned out to be amazing at writing. If you give your staff the space and opportunity to develop, you never know what talents you can unleash.

---

[22] N. Botterill, 'Recruiting superstars: A how to guide to hiring the best staff', *RealBusiness* (31 May 2016). Available from: www.realbusiness.co.uk/recruiting-superstars-a-how-to-guide-to-hiring-the-best-staff

Tip No. 5

Although they are most often amazing, I'd be aware that hiring friends to work in your business, can sometimes cause friction and could create problems when the work finishes, as there is always an underlying tone which ends up ruining the original friendship.

Tip No. 6

Young people love technology, so I have developed our own staff website for supporting and training staff and providing them with information. I thrashed out in excess of 150 questions and answers and put them all on there. There are numerous training videos, staff policies and procedures, and employment guidance – staff also have access to the Staff Experience Fund through the website. It's worth investing in creating a good website to support your staff (obviously depending upon the size of your team).

Tip No. 7

We find that the best way to communicate with staff is to use Facebook. We have a private Facebook group dedicated to the staff where we post information about events, rotas and important communications.

Tip No. 8

We also use the Entrepreneurs Circle's 'What does 100% look like' as part of our appraisal process, where we ask staff to answer four questions:

1. What are you doing when you are performing at 100% in your role?
2. What do you need from the business in order to be able to perform at that level?
3. What should your reward be when you are performing at that level?
4. What should the ramifications be when you don't perform at that level?

Tip No. 9

I try to make working at The Wellbeing Farm fun for staff and to give them as many experiences as possible to enhance their CVs. Together with the staff we have developed and implemented the Staff Experience Fund, whereby for every wedding booked from 1 January 2019 onwards, £xxx will be paid into the new team fund. The funds will be used throughout the year in a variety of ways and the staff decide how the money should be spent. The fund is used in the following ways:

- To fund team-building and away days
- Staff parties and nights out
- Initiatives to support staff 'wellbeing' e.g. sponsored runs, health days, yoga classes
- To support staff participation in sporting events
- Treats, such as sweets, for the office and staff corridor
- Rewards for 'Star of the Month'.

Other ways of motivating staff are to have a Star of the Month, where the winning employee is rewarded with an Amazon voucher. We also have a staff suggestion scheme whereby staff members are rewarded for any idea they propose that we subsequently implement.

Tip No. 10

Have regular staff communication and coordination meetings. Traction proposes a new style of meeting called the 'Level 10 meeting' which we have adapted and implemented in our business, as explained in Chapter 5.

Tip No. 11

Don't delay firing someone if it's clear that things aren't working out. Hospitality is all about customer service and communication, and I am pleased to say that attitudes of our staff and their personalities are the things for which I receive the most compliments. I absolutely love seeing staff develop their skills, communication and abilities through working at the farm and will always try to give them new skills and challenges to enhance their CVs. During the summer months, we deliver a considerable number of weddings which require staff to work long hours, remain calm under a huge amount of pressure and maintain a pleasant customer-facing disposition at all times. All staff demonstrate considerable professional stamina, a commitment to and a capacity for hard work, and an ability to perform under pressure with excellent resilience skills. The fact that I use staff of all ages to help showcase the venue to new customers, knowing that the staff's enthusiasm for the venue is a key selling point in itself, is testimony to the amazing team I have in place.

Over to you...

- Every vision needs a team who supports that vision to make it a reality.
- It is up to you as the business owner to find and recruit the right people for your team, to communicate your vision and to invest in building and sustaining your team's skills, attitude, enthusiasm, energy and willingness to succeed.

PART THREE

Building your resilience – how to survive and your personal support

Chapter 8

Yes, it can all get out of control...

....

The very first company I started failed with a great bang. The second one failed a little bit less, but still failed. The third one, you know, proper failed, but it was kind of OK. I recovered quickly. Number four almost didn't fail. It still didn't really feel great, but it did OK. Number five was PayPal.

Max Levchin

....

I n this chapter I want to outline how my enthusiasm got the better of me and what I had to do to survive. I hope my story will resonate with business owners and individuals in showing how sometimes you can be on a particular path only to find that you need to adapt and change.

I had never managed a construction project in my life. From the moment I opened, there was a huge burden of debt. I had borrowed against Stephen's farm – the building work overran (I eventually opened in March 2013) and with a project like this, especially for corporate events, you need photos etc. to market and promote the venue. There was always going to be a three to six month lag before getting any business from corporate bookings.

My enthusiasm started to run away with me. I started a café at the farm and tried to attract people to come to the café. I started a petting farm and I started school visits and I started courses and I started the next thing... I ended up running 14 different subsidiaries from the farm: corporate events and a training centre, llama trekking, wellbeing centre, lifestyle courses, café, cookery school, butchery courses, large-scale events, children's parties, petting farm, school visits, afternoon teas, parties and weddings – the road map looked like this:

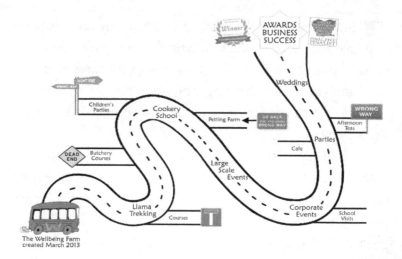

It's embedded in the nature of entrepreneurs to take risks, to try new ideas, to be agile. But you need to understand how to balance the need to experiment with the need to be rigorous and stop doing things that don't work or have stopped working – all in the context of not taking on too much at any one time.

Just how do you keep going when times are tough? I did come close to packing it all in.

It was on 5 August 2014 that Victor Giannandrea (my mentor) first made contact with me via email. I was introduced to Victor via Community & Business Partners CIC (www.cbpartners.org) – a non-profit-making organisation established to support businesses, community groups and voluntary bodies with a range of services, both advisory and practical.

With a promise of scones being available, Victor arranged to visit the farm on 6 August 2014 and when I met him I was in a very bad place – struggling financially, confused and overwhelmed. Victor's words to me were, 'It was terrific meeting you and the Team yesterday, you certainly have the solid foundations of a good business. The business isn't broken, it's just got a bit foggy and complicated with lots of tasks that need prioritising, we just need to focus on some of the more crucial important issues. It would be very helpful if we could "harness your enthusiasm and energy".'

We set about putting a plan of action into place. Victor made me realise that I had failed to focus on the two things that make you successful as a business:

- Recruit, retain and manage people.
- Manage the cash.

I read an online article written by James Cox called 'It's all in the positioning'[23] which was pivotal to me and made me realise what had gone wrong… That article changed everything.

Originally I had spent months and months thinking about and planning the concept of The Wellbeing Farm and I had done a lot of research to develop that concept. I had visited 196 similar businesses around the country and I was very clear about what I wanted The Wellbeing Farm to look like. This was presented to the bank via a very comprehensive business plan and I believed I had developed a unique concept. I was clear in my business plan what services I was going to offer, what my methodology would be and how much cash I would need.

---

[23] J. Cox, 'It's all in the positioning: What to do when your business seems to be losing focus', *SmallBusiness* (26 June 2014). Available from: https://smallbusiness.co.uk/its-all-in-the-positioning-what-to-do-when-your-business-seems-to-be-losing-focus-2465692/

This is where the problems started...

The building work was originally scheduled to end in December 2012. This would have given me three months to finish the work, organise the processes and procedures, and prepare for the press launch. I had originally organised a high-flying press launch for the farm for March 2013. As it happened, the building work overran by eight weeks, so when the time came I had to proceed with the launch but it meant that I never got the three-month period I had planned to organise the processes and procedures.

The press launch in March 2013 was a huge event which escalated the profile of The Wellbeing Farm – people thought it was an amazing concept. Everyone wanted access to the farm, but I had never intended for it to be used by the general public. However, pressure was mounting for me to open up the farm to the public... this is why when I read James Cox's article one passage really resonated with me:

> *Then when your first whiff of an actual, paying client comes along, you say yes even though they've asked you to do something a little outside your original plan. It's an irresistible temptation. Especially if you're a creative thinker (like most start-ups and small business leaders). And especially if you're focused on generating income (again we all are at this stage of*

> *business growth). Every time it happens then the*
> *further out the window your carefully honed plan*
> *goes.*[24]

That carefully constructed plan that I had spent months and months creating and developing was overnight thrown out of the window and replaced by me doing things which were never in the original business plan…

Opening a café for example. I realised that by opening the café, the uniqueness and specialness of The Wellbeing Farm had gone. The premium prices that people would pay to access the farm (in terms of corporate events and functions) had disappeared and been replaced by a model which offered bacon sandwiches and pies – this was never my vision.

I had ended up with a business which was unfocused; I had no clarity in what I was offering (especially to corporates), people didn't know what The Wellbeing Farm offered or even did – the whole business was confusing.

> *Suddenly it is a year later and you find that you've*
> *spread yourself too thin. Your original vision and the*
> *value you aimed to provide are not focused on that*
> *special sweet spot you had identified at all. Instead*
> *you are doing a whole host of things for your customers*

---

[24] Cox, 'It's all in the positioning'.

that you never intended or wanted to. Your margins are slipping and you're not enjoying it so much. After all, you can't be an expert at everything. You see your differentiator, based on your original proposition, slowly slipping away.[25]

That is exactly what had happened to me…

It was at that moment that I realised it was time to get my head out of the sand and start sorting it out.

I needed to re-focus and get my plans back on track.

I pressed the pause button on 22 December 2014 and took time away from my business to work *on* it, not *in* it – this was one of the most worthwhile things I've done. It left me feeling re-energised, and while this sort of change is never easy, the benefits are enormous.

I dug out my original business plan and reviewed it – except this time I was 18 months wiser about running a business. I was upset at reading it – realising how far I had drifted from my original business plan and wondering why I had allowed myself to do this.

So, here I was in December 2014, facing potential bankruptcy over an £8,000 VAT bill – the full story of which is told in Chapter 4 – but with a kind of

---

[25] Cox, 'It's all in the positioning'.

inkling that people liked the venue for weddings. Then something amazing happened which saved my business. Something I had never even thought of. You see, my dad had left a bag full of bow ties – being a concert pianist and organist, he obviously had many. I remember laughing with my mum about what on earth she was going to do with all these bow ties. I said to her, 'Do you know what, I feel like putting a bow tie on a llama.'

This bag of bow ties meant I could try bow ties on the llamas and not worry about the expense if they didn't fit. I would just put the bow tie on the llama and see what happened. The llamas had the perfect necks. They're very long and straight and suit a bow tie.

The pivotal moment when things began to change was the day that I put one of my dad's bow ties on a Llama. We leapt from two weddings in 2014 to 15 in 2015 and 43 in 2016 and we continued to grow. My business became different. My business stood out. It had something that no other business had. My business had bow-tie-wearing llamas.

Figure 8.1: The bow-tie-wearing llamas
(Photo credit: Shane Webber Photography)

That was the start of the transformation of my business. Up to that point, The Wellbeing Farm was just another venue, but the bow-tie-wearing llamas meant we suddenly became a venue that stood out. We became a venue that differentiated itself from all the other competition and yes, somebody else could go and get llamas, but it takes a long time to train a llama to be able to mingle with you and your guests over a drink. People's reaction said it all – 'What on earth is a llama doing at a wedding?' Some guests have never even seen a llama – you normally only ever see them in petting farms or zoos and then they've got a reputation for spitting (they rarely spit at humans by the way).

So putting a bow tie on a llama literally changed my business overnight. The moral of the story is that whatever awful things happen to you in life, with the right attitude something good will always come out of it.

Over to you...

- What's your crazy idea?
- What's the catalyst that makes you want to change the road you are on?
- Do you suffer from 'shiny-object' syndrome and always want to do more, rather than focusing on the key developments that will fundamentally change your life and business?
- Do you suffer from fear of missing out?

Chapter 9

How do you know your crazy idea will work? Being brave

Your work is going to fill a large part of your life, and the only way to be truly satisfied is to do what you believe is great work. And the only way to do great work is to love what you do.

Steve Jobs

When you set up a business and it's up and running, things will happen, things will go wrong and it's how you recover from setbacks (your bouncebackability) and how resilient you are that leads to business success or failure.

In this chapter I describe some of the things that have happened to me – things I wish people had warned me about – so, as the saying goes, to be forewarned is to be forearmed. You need to overcome these elements, develop and master your entrepreneurial skills and learn to embrace failure.

While riding my entrepreneurial rollercoaster, I feel I've had more than my fair share of setbacks, but I've developed a fighting spirit – you have to. In this section

I outline some of the challenges you may face and some strategies for overcoming them.

The most critical thing is to buy yourself a hard-backed business journal and document your journey – you never know, you might want to write your story into a book.

You might read this book and be thinking 'How stupid of you.' But nobody told me. There wasn't a road map saying, 'This is how you transform a farm.' The experiences you read in this book weren't theoretical, they are my story based on the memories and facts of what actually happened. Success isn't about what you accomplish in your life, it's about what you inspire others to do. When you read this book, I want you to be inspired to do something to transform your life or business and I hope this book will help you to do this.

Starting out

During this pre-business phase, these are the key challenges to look out for.

The doubters

These are the people who will say how silly your idea is. 'Stick with your current job; you'll get a good pension etc.' You've got to believe in your idea, what will happen if you don't do it – what will your death-bed experience look like? I love thinking back on the people who ridiculed me when I said I was going to purchase some llamas – look at how popular llamas are today!

Get to know your neighbours and seek support for your plans

Their opinions will be critical when you are seeking planning permission. Connect with your local Chamber of Commerce (www.britishchambers.org.uk) and the Federation of Small Businesses (www.fsb.org.uk), attend business networking events and generate contacts – it's who you know that always counts. As I described in Chapter 3, key contacts are critical, especially in the face of the upsetting and frustrating problems I experienced. Also, be careful if you have tenants on your farm or anyone that is renting your property – you may need to serve them notice.

Test your plans

It is difficult to set up a wedding venue from scratch. If you already have a venue or a farm, test your concept as I described in Chapter 3. This is a great way to test your market and also develop some early photos of your venue.

Developing your business case

Don't make the mistake of creating a 50-page business plan like I did. If you are seeking finance, anyone lending you money is going to want to see a robust and focused case for their financial investment. You will also need a project plan/road map to follow. There are some really good templates you can use in the online resources section of my website (www.celiagaze.com); you should also follow the advice in Chapter 2.

Planning permission

Anticipate that planning permission is going to be the delaying factor and one of the most frustrating elements of your journey. If you are in a greenbelt area, I would just go straight to someone who specialises in rural planning consultancy to seek their opinions – it may cost you, but it will save you heartache, delays and so much frustration. Make sure you take transport and car parking into consideration from the outset – much more detail on all these elements can be found in Chapter 3.

Designing your vision

If you are going to diversify your farm or existing building, you must seek help from an architect with experience of commercial projects to help you with your plans. They will know the regulations around the number of toilets, fire exits, disability requirements etc. which you will need to incorporate – cutting corners in these areas will cost you in the long term, so embrace and incorporate these elements at an early stage. Learn from the problems I experienced, which are described in Chapter 3.

Raising finance

I'm pleased to say that with organisations like Funding Circle, raising finance is so much easier now than it was eight years ago. I was rejected by five banks before I secured the money to convert the farm. I remember appealing to one bank who fed back to me that I didn't know how to write a business plan and that I shouldn't have submitted a five-year forecast. I'm sure that in your area there are organisations like the one I used, Access to Finance. Access to Finance is a government-backed initiative aimed at helping those who have been rejected by banks to find finance, and their advice was free of charge. You just need to find your local equivalent to help you – your accountant will usually be a good starting point. Further information and details on this can be found in Chapter 4.

Think about how you will control your cash flow

In Chapter 4, I outlined the problems I faced around business rates and VAT. Set up your bank accounts as I have advised and make sure from the outset that you are protecting funds for your VAT bill. Similarly, try to get an idea of your business rates before starting out so that you can budget for these. Remember that cash flow is your number one priority and cash flow problems have the power to make or break your business.

Set up your own risk register

Hopefully this book will help you to think about all the things which could go wrong (your weaknesses and threats) and about ways you could prevent these risks from happening. You need to face your fears and map all the problems out so that you are prepared for the worst should it happen. Then put some actions together on how you will overcome them with some timescales. This exercise will help reduce stress and give you peace of mind.

Manage your project

I had a project/programme management background combined with an MBA. I had won a judicial review in the High Court of London, but I found the whole process of setting up a business a huge challenge. You really need to thrash out everything you need to do into some sort of plan with key dates, milestones and targets to reach. Think about the risks you face and seek to address your weaknesses through learning and attending relevant courses.

The build or the creation stage

You've secured your finances and your permissions, you are creating your dream – here are some of the things you need to think about.

Sales and marketing

Get some architect drawings/impressions drawn up to be able to sell your venue. Most couples will get your vision, so don't be afraid of showing people your plans. Keep taking photographs to seek early marketing engagement and buy-in – people will love seeing your vision develop and will begin to follow your story. Couples fell in love with our venue, even when it didn't even have toilets, because they saw the potential. They will be really impressed and will enjoy watching it evolve into a stunning venue. This is the way to develop your know, like and trust factor which will be critical for the future.

Regulations

Seek early input from the fire brigade, environmental health, licensing and Building Regulations – don't leave these until the last minute. Build these relationships as they will be critical when you open, and you can overcome delays and unexpected outcomes if these key areas have been considered in your designs and projects – see Chapter 5 for further details.

Keep control of your building costs

You should obtain a quote from your builder at the very beginning, and then ask for regular updates on how costs are proceeding against that original quote. I would allow for a 25% contingency fund to allow for extra and unexpected building costs.

Support your family and friends

Your dream will become time consuming and it will take over – for you it is exciting and exhilarating, for others it can seem dominating and something which is chipping away at your relationships. It is critical that you maintain your relationships – you will need them more than ever when you start trading and the ride really does become bumpier.

Your operating processes and procedures

The types of areas you need to think about are explored in Chapter 5 and within the online resources. I remember in my early days a couple booked a party and the woman turned up wearing a wedding dress (presumably they were trying to get a cheap wedding). I've had heated discussions with couples who refused to pay before their wedding day. It is absolutely critical that while your venue is being designed you are thinking about all these areas and documenting them, with robust terms and conditions so that everyone is clear on these from the outset. There are so many things you are going to need to think about, including pricing, how you will run your venue, contracts you will need to have in place (such as booking terms and conditions), how you will accept payments, appointment systems, who will be providing the catering and drinks, and how you will clean the venue. Unfortunately the list does become endless but I've attempted to highlight the things you need to consider in Chapter 5 and within the online resources. Remember to be clear on your terms and conditions – there are plenty of people out there that will try to take advantage of you.

When you start trading

Sales and marketing
This is critical – without sales there is no income. You must put the bulk of your energy into this. Stage things like photoshoots to showcase your venue and show people what your weddings will be like. There are loads of companies who will organise a wedding fair at your venue free of charge to attract much-needed awareness and publicity. Embrace social media and document your journey as much as possible. Keep writing in that business journal. Sales and marketing need to be your highest priority – do not skimp on sales or marketing spend – this brings in business which in turn brings you income. The ability to get customers is the most fundamental part of your business.

Set up your bank accounts
It's so easy to spend money as soon as it comes in. When income is received, protect your VAT payments and overheads and then use the remaining money to run your business.

Be staff prepared
Employing staff is one of the biggest costs in running a business, so you need to ensure that you have the right systems, processes and procedures in place to ensure that you comply with employment legislation and also that you make the most of your staff assets.

Things will happen

I remember 1 March 2018 as a particularly bad day. Storm Emma – otherwise known as the 'Beast from the East' – had arrived, and we were due to host a wedding the next day. We had no water and snow had drifted all the way up the drive – it was so bad that only a digger could dig us out of the farm. We had to search for emergency grit as all our grit supplies had been depleted, there was a flood in the kitchen, the dog ran off, there were 90-mph winds and a –15-degree wind chill factor. On top of all this, my wedding coordinator decided to resign. You will face days like this and it's all about how you cope with the challenges.

Be different

To survive in a competitive environment you have got to be different. You've got to find something that makes you stand out from the crowd. Be a flamingo in a flock of pigeons – stand out, be different and be unique.

Don't go too overboard with the decor

Many couples start developing their Pinterest board as soon as they get engaged, using it as a platform to document their vision, enthusiasm and excitement for their big day. Most couples therefore want a neutral, blank canvas – an adaptable space with endless potential. Couples love letting their imaginations run wild and you need to allow them to do that.

Seek to have fabulous customer service from the outset

We have gone out of our way to create a wedding venue that was not only different, but which embraced customer service from the beginning. Taking the principles of wellbeing, I describe in Chapter 2 how I sought to apply these to the venue design. This has since expanded to us providing not just a venue, but also a supportive wedding planning system to our couples. Known as the SHAPE Wedding Planning System, our support covers five areas which I explain in detail in Chapter 5.

Be aware though that your support can go too far. The colour of the carpet we had laid in the wedding barn was always a bone of contention. Too light and every single stain showed up – and when you are serving bottles and bottles of red wine and people are dancing, spillages can easily happen. Similarly, if the carpet was too dark it just looked dreary. At the time I was embracing wedding trends, and bringing the outside in was a huge trend at the time, so I got carried away and thought it would be a great idea to have a green carpet – how wrong that proved to be! Couples want a blank-canvas wedding venue. They will base their wedding plans around this, sometimes choosing a bold vivid colour scheme to contrast against the rustic feel of the barn. I quickly had to replace the carpet for the same coloured carpet I had previously had in place, at a huge cost to the business.

Today I face other challenges – unfortunately my health has suffered at the expense of my business and my focus today is on my health, writing this book and allowing the farm to continue to grow. The pressure still remains, but I am wiser, stronger, more adaptable and most importantly I have learned to embrace failure. I have used my failures and experiences of darker times in a positive way – I reflected, adapted and learned from them. I am now documenting them in the hope that my learning will have the same effect on you.

Bravery comes down to being prepared, embracing failure, being resilient and your bouncebackability – these are the skills I will highlight in the next chapter.

Over to you…

- Never give up – when you feel like quitting just remember why you started.
- There will be bumps on your entrepreneurial road, but that doesn't mean it's the end – learn from your mistakes and the hurdles you encounter and use them to implement processes and systems which will avoid the same pitfalls in the future.
- Learn to embrace failure – do it again and again and again and learn that failure is all part of success. Sometimes there isn't always a good strategy, but as long as you are willing to educate yourself, fail fast and then learn from your mistakes, this will stand you in good stead for the future.

Chapter 10

The skills you will need to develop to survive

....

When you reach an obstacle, turn it into an opportunity. You have the choice. You can overcome and be a winner, or you can allow it to overcome you and be a loser. The choice is yours and yours alone. Refuse to throw in the towel. Go that extra mile that failures refuse to travel. It is far better to be exhausted from success than to be rested from failure.

Mary Kay Ash

....

There are different skills you will need to succeed and these will depend upon your own personal perspective and background. The skills will be different if you are an entrepreneur, facing a mid-life crisis, a farmer who wants to understand how to diversify his/her land, or a wedding planner running a venue.

During your entrepreneurial journey there are skills that you will need to develop – some you will already have and some you are going to have to learn. Some you can learn by attending a course, but many unfortunately you will need to learn the hard way, through direct experience. Many skills are developed personally by adopting a positive mental state through self-care. In this chapter, I describe my journey of personal transformation to develop these skills.

From my direct experience in documenting my journey, I believe the key ingredients for success are as follows.

Accountability

I like accountability and I like working with plans and deadlines. I just couldn't get into my writing until my publisher gave me a deadline. Accountability and planning involving deadlines is important. The main purpose of accountability is to keep your work and progress towards a specific goal at the forefront of your mind. Having the right accountability partner (someone who will keep you on track with your goals) is also important and that's where a mentor can be invaluable. A good mentor is someone who has 'done it and got the t-shirt'; they leave their ego at the door. They have the scars to prove their explanations and skills. What's the difference between a mentor and a coach? In mentoring the learner sets their own goals, whereas a coach usually sets goals for the learner. Both sources of support need to be good listeners and respect the confidentiality of the learner.

Over to you…
- Who keeps you accountable?
- Do you have your goals documented with timescales for achievement?
- How do you stay on track?

Bouncebackability

This can also be described as resilience, persistence and positivity. Things are going to go wrong, so be expected to fail many times – but the difference between a successful business owner and an unsuccessful business owner is how you cope with the difficult times. I could have lost my business in December 2014; however, I was forced to reflect, adapt, reduce the number of activities I was doing and transform.

Over to you…
- To be successful you need to be able to adapt and change quickly. Change needs to be perceived as a positive thing.
- When you start feeling that everything is against you, take a step back, get some rest, connect, nurture yourself, clear your head and start again. If being successful was easy, no one would ever fail. At times you will experience difficulties and you will need to remain positive and face your struggles – it's out of the hard times that we rise strong and fierce.

Create the magic

Think about how your business will become the flamingo amongst a flock of pigeons. People will pay more for a unique experience. How are you going to do the equivalent of putting the bow tie on the llama?

Over to you...

- Passion has to be your driving force and you can use this to love what you do so much that you want to do more of it; the more you do it, the more magical it becomes.
- What is your equivalent of putting a bow tie on a llama?

Personal development

Never stop learning – 100+ courses later and I vow to never stop learning, I learn something new every day and I am constantly reading, devouring as many business books as I can. Having an MBA just isn't enough. The courses I have attended so far include gift wrapping, pizza making, time management, soap making, abstract art, interior design, sculpture, pottery, life drawing, yoga, pilates, calligraphy, floristry, flower arranging, sewing, llama care, alpaca care, donkey care, wedding planning, meditation, mindfulness, decluttering, puppy training, salsa, DIY, car maintenance, Spanish, reflexology,

Ayurveda, stress management, emotional intelligence, organisational management, project management, programme management, upholstery, picture framing, presentation skills, book writing, NLP, bookkeeping, and law of attraction, to name just some of the courses I have attended. These courses have shaped my business, strengthened my mindset and given me credibility, creativity and much more. This is why I am so passionate about personal development.

> **Over to you…**
>
> • Personal development as an entrepreneur is really important – the more you read, experience and see, the more you understand what other people are doing.
> • The only thing that no one can take away from you is your knowledge.
> • What courses do you need to do to strengthen your mindset and learning?

Planning and resourcefulness

You've got to put the effort in to fully understand your vision and the risks you are taking as well as the opportunities. You can develop a perfect business plan, but sometimes you've also got to be very good at adaptability. You have got to be prepared to change direction and embrace opportunities – weddings didn't even feature in my original business plan.

Over to you...

- Be ready to work and change whatever needs to be done differently.
- Plan for both the worst and the best possible outcomes and revise your business plan on a regular basis.
- Remember that all big jobs are just little ones in a row. Breaking things down into small steps makes them so much more manageable and much less overwhelming.
- Cash flow is critical.

Processes

Learn to love processes and systems; they are critical in the effective running of a business. Documented processes bring you freedom. Start documenting your processes right at the beginning, get your team involved and develop your operations manual. As a business owner, you should be able to go on holiday and relax – truly relax – because your operations manual is in place.

> ## Over to you...
>
> - Create and use systems consistently.
> - Start early on and document the processes as you learn them.
> - What systems and processes have you already developed which you can start documenting?
> - Processes and systems bring you (the business owner) freedom.

Productivity

You've got to be good at meeting deadlines; your time is precious so manage it well. I thrive on productivity and, at the time of writing this book, won the title of Implementer of the Year at the National Entrepreneur Awards in the Get S**t Done category. Implement productivity techniques such as batched working and bite-sized chunks, and learn to say no to things you might feel obliged to do. Nigel Botterill is a massive advocate of the '90 Minutes a Day' way of working,[26] and this is heavily promoted by his association, the Entrepreneurs Circle. 90 minutes for you. 90 minutes of pure switch-your-phone-off concentrated effort, doing, growing and

---

[26] N. Botterill and M. Gladdish, *Building Your Business in 90 Minutes a Day* (2015).

working *on* your business rather than *in* it. 90 minutes of just pure time – you need that time to grow your business.

90-day goals

My business runs on 90-day goals – 90 days to drive significant progress and implementation which all members of the business deliver. The whole business is driven, focused and enthusiastic, and this is demonstrated in our 90-day plans. The goals we set are what we need to constantly grow our business.

The One Thing

I love the book *The One Thing* by Garry Keller.[27] So many Facebook posts in groups say something like 'What is the one thing you could do this week to shift your business forward?' or 'What is the one thing you are going to set out to achieve this week?' It's true that often when I'm stuck or feeling overwhelmed I resort to the One Thing philosophy to simplify everything I've got to do. When I'm feeling particularly overwhelmed or I've got a big deadline, I really focus to get things done. **I use hotels in quite unusual ways to achieve the One Thing** – at least a couple of times each month I pack up my desk and check

---

[27] G. Keller with J. Papasan, *The One Thing: The Surprisingly Simple Truth Behind Extraordinary Results* (2014).

into a twin room for preferably two nights. I use one bed to sleep in, of course, and the other bed I use basically as a massive desk. I ask the hotel to give me an early check in and a late check out, then I spread everything out on my 'desk' and I do not leave the room.

Now the great thing about working in hotels is (1) you've got no cleaning because they even come and make your bed (!) and (2) you can have breakfast on-site and you also don't have to cook your evening meals. It doesn't have to be a luxurious hotel by any means; in fact, the more basic the better because you're not tempted to go out of the room. You do not want a hotel where there are loads of extra facilities because these are just a distraction. You need to lock yourself away and just get on with the work. Now, if they have some nice grounds outside you can go out and get some fresh air, but you shouldn't check into a hotel in a big town with loads of shops because these will just distract you. I lock myself away, turning off my emails and my phone so I'm basically non-contactable, and I crack on with getting big pieces of work done and completed with no distractions. That is how I've been able to achieve so much – by locking myself away and focusing on the one thing I need to do to drive my business forward. Writing in hotels and locking myself away is how I wrote this book! The One Thing proves that focusing intently and deliberately on getting one thing done at a time is far more productive than trying to do everything at once.

Early morning working

My golden time to get work done (and this is another key to how I get so much done) is 4am to 7am – the internet is fantastic; nobody disturbs you at that time (they are generally all asleep). I can achieve so much by working early in the morning. Nigel Botterill's book[28] advocates dedicating 90 minutes every day to growing your business, working on personal development and undertaking marketing, and I try and achieve this every day during my early morning working time. The 4–7am slot is my equivalent of the 90 minutes to make things happen.

Over to you...

- What's your big vision? Where do you want your business to be in 10 years' time?
- What is the business going to look like three years from now?
- What is the business going to look like one year from now?
- Break your one-year goal into 90-day chunks to create quarterly goals. What do you want to make happen in the next 90 days?

---

[28] Botterill and Gladdish, *Building Your Business*.

- What goals are you setting for yourself?
- How are you going to plan to achieve your goals? You need to prioritise and be clear on your top priorities.
- You'll never get rid of the 'To Do' list, so you need to find ways of bringing productivity into your life. I've shared some of my tips; what can you think of doing to make yourself more productive?

Seek support

Sometimes you have to acknowledge that you don't know the answers and you've got to seek help. I spent weeks sourcing every bit of support I could get, and you'll understand from reading this book how valuable a mentor could become to you. You've got to be honest, tenacious and not afraid to seek knowledge. However, remember that sometimes things are too good to be true – don't trust those people who claim to save you thousands of pounds in business rates, be wary of website developers who don't need a contract and always obtain three quotes for everything. Be wary of those difficult members of staff you will encounter. Become the leader who inspires them and brings their team with them.

When you are in business, it can be lonely. There are things that you don't want to talk to other business owners or your staff about. Your friends are bored of you constantly talking about your business and your partner switched off long ago. That's when a mentor is invaluable. I have shared more about my business with Victor than with anyone else – he has critiqued responses to couples who were cancelling their wedding, helped with difficult staffing issues and supported me through legal challenges and financial shortfalls. I believe a good mentor is essential for your mental survival.

Over to you...

- Understand that you'll always feel behind as you'll always be aware that there's more to learn.
- Try to start building a team as quickly as possible – having even a little help goes a long way.
- Create your own support network, as not everyone will get or support you. Believe in yourself.
- Pay for expertise whenever you can – don't struggle to do everything yourself.

Self-belief

My self-belief was demonstrated to its fullest when I had to confront the tenant living on Stephen's farm. A year after I met Stephen, we both had our own houses. Stephen rented out his farmhouse but kept control of the livery business. The tenant approached Stephen one day asking whether he could take over management of the livery business, to which he agreed. The problem came when we wanted to develop the farm – because the tenant was now effectively running a business from the farm (the livery business) and Stephen hadn't thought of putting a business lease in place (just the lease associated with the farmhouse), trying to get the tenant off the farm was very difficult.

An essential and critical component of being a successful business owner is to have the support of people who believe in you. As much as I love my mum, at the beginning I did get a lot of, 'Well Celia, you've given up that NHS pension, here you are facing these problems and why on earth are you bothering doing this? Go back to the NHS; they'll welcome you.' You do sometimes think about the choices you've made and you question 'Is this worth all of this?' Even Stephen at one point said, 'Well Celia, is this worth all of this?' You've got to keep going and believing that it will happen, although at times it is very, very difficult, especially when you have that type of family pressure on you. I had put up all this money up-front and we weren't getting any returns, and I needed more and more money to survive.

Over to you…

- Mindset is critical. You need bucket-loads of faith and a tonne of patience coupled with a loving and supportive family/spouse. Setting up a business will test the strength of your relationships and you've got to help your partner get something out of your dream too.
- The business journey is a marathon, not a sprint; don't compare someone's six-year journey to your six-month one. Have the belief in yourself that you can achieve what you set out to do and acknowledge where you are at and be grateful for it.
- Self-belief and self-trust really are crucial to everything.
- We all have to start somewhere and it's only natural to feel uncertain in a job you've never done before. Don't let your lack of experience or lack of knowledge keep you from trying. Just try. Try that crazy idea you've always had – just keep pursuing, keep creating and keep going. Stop thinking what others will think – just go for it!

Slow down

I've done a lot of reading lately on the benefits of going slow, such as the Slow Hustle approach created by Peter

Awad (www.peterawad.com) and '**go slow to grow**' is my mantra for 2019. You see, prior to this I'd been behaving like this super busy, crazy woman. I was finding that I was in this game of constantly juggling full plates of work, endless chores, places to be and things to do. I was never off my phone, responding to emails and joining more and more Facebook groups, which actually creates constant pressure in itself. To save time I would wolf down my meals in a hurry and not get enough sleep, thinking that if I had less sleep I would have time to do more. I was neglecting time for friends and family and I forgot how to sit idle and do nothing. As a result, my mind was unable to be still, to be quiet and therefore to slow down, and I realised that my mind and body were just not getting enough time to recharge and recover.

I had become obsessed with how much I'd accomplished and how fast I'd done it and I was seeing this as a measure of success. Then I started to question why I was always in such a rush. The pressure for constant growth had meant I had ended up with a 'go, go, go' mentality that leaves little room for reflection and planning. Instead I was constantly pushing for newer and bigger markets, new products etc. So I vowed that 2019 would be the year that I took time to slow down, reflect, think, plan, focus and refine – the tortoise has become my symbol for 2019.

A study in *Harvard Business Review* found that companies that chose to 'go, go, go' without thinking through their business strategy ended up with lower sales and operating profits than those that 'paused at key moments to make sure they were on the right track.'[29] Companies that took this slow and deliberate strategic approach ended up averaging 40% higher sales and 52% higher operating profits. Business owners that slow down and help their management team through a strategic planning process often find more success in the long run as they bring their team together, agree key priorities and goals, explain the reasons why decisions are being made, listen to feedback and get everyone aligned with their plans.

There are also huge knock-on benefits to your team if you slow down – instead of always rushing, slowing down allows you to build the strong company culture which is essential for a business to grow and survive. I am terrible for talking too quickly and rarely wait for the other person to finish or end up talking over them. When I communicate slowly it helps me to put the thoughts of the other person first. When I'm rushing I make

---

[29] J. R. Davis and T. Atkinson, 'Need Speed? Slow Down'. *Harvard Business Review* (May 2010). Available from: https://hbr.org/2010/05/need-speed-slow-down

mistakes, make poor decisions, misjudge and misread situations, and get caught up in reactive firefighting rather than productively moving forward on what really matters. When I slow myself down – walk slower, talk slower, take slower deeper breaths – my clarity of thought returns. I've found that doing daily morning meditation and yoga has really helped me in this respect.

Over to you…

- What's your pace of work like?
- What are you going to introduce into your life to enable you to cope with the demands of entrepreneurship?
- Do you need to embrace techniques to slow down and become more mindful?

Vision

You've got to be creative – who would ever have imagined that a horse arena could become an award-wining wedding venue, that llamas would wear bow ties, that military parachutes would form an amazing ceiling for a venue? You've got to be creative, think outside of the box and not be afraid of doing something which may seem really crazy at the outset.

Over to you...
Visualise exactly what you want out of your life or your business and do everything and anything you can to get it. Keep focused on the end result.

As I've already mentioned, at the beginning there will be loads of people who will think your crazy idea is stupid – you've got to be determined to succeed and develop your self-belief, perseverance and resilience. It's about being prepared for all the risks and having an appetite for risk. Keep thinking about your death-bed scene and how you want to feel and just do it. Life is too short for regrets.

Chapter 11

How your crazy idea can grow a bigger life

So that morning in 1962 I told myself: Let everyone else call your idea crazy… just keep going. Don't stop. Don't even think about stopping until you get there, and don't give much thought to where 'there' is. Whatever comes, just don't stop. That's the precious, prescient, urgent advice I managed to give myself, out of the blue, and somehow managed to take. Half a century later, I believe it's the best advice – maybe the only advice – any of us should ever give.

P. Knight, *Shoe Dog: A Memoir by the Creator of Nike* (2016)

So how do you cope?

As I was writing this book, I was forced to look back and relive the stories about business rates, inspectors, planning permission, rejection, near bankruptcy, credit card debt and having to write letters to my mum. I was in tears writing this book at times and you may not believe me when I describe what I went through to transform the farm, but I did go through all those things and survived to tell the tale. By writing this book I have had to reflect and learn more about myself than I could ever imagine.

So how did I cope? What were, and are, my personal survival tactics?

Entrepreneurship is exhilarating and exciting and there are so many benefits to running your own business, such as flexibility, giving yourself permission to change the world and pursue your dreams, doing fulfilling work – you have a purpose to drive you every day. However, on the other hand entrepreneurs work long hours, have a lack of 'me time', often burn the candle at both ends, don't take breaks and can suffer from mental exhaustion. I know my current ways of crazy working will eventually lead to burnout. I am on the road to burnout with a diagnosis of pre-diabetes. I have red hair and I'm an Aries; as a result I'm feisty and I struggle to control my emotions. I realise that as a business owner your reputation depends on your professionalism and your ability to manage your emotions, whatever challenges you face. Lashing out in anger, crying uncontrollably when things get too much or harbouring resentment are all areas I need to control, and are all made worse by overwork and stress.

I've been guilty of prioritising my work over my health and this definitely needs to change. According to Bronnie Ware in her book *The Top Five Regrets of the*

Dying, 'from the moment you lose your health, it is too late. Health brings a freedom very few realise, until they no longer have it.'[30]

So don't make the mistakes I made – learn from them.

One of the reasons for my long working hours was linked to living on the farm – I could never switch off. The exhilaration, fun and pure joy of living on the farm doing something I loved on a day-to-day basis meant I found it hard to switch off.

So, in April 2019, we moved house and returned to my lovely home in the village of Turton, and in May 2019 I decided to take a month off my business and to go travelling and on a yoga retreat in Bali and Australia. I am proud to say that I took a proper break and survived for four weeks without email! I'm delighted to say that while I was away, my business grew, my staff were empowered and when I returned my work life balance was very different.

In my quest for the perfect entrepreneurial life-style I have read numerous books on the health of the entrepreneur and I have found things that have helped me cope. In this chapter I will share the coping mechanisms that have begun to transform my life and

---

[30] B. Ware, *The Top Five Regrets of the Dying: A Life Transformed by the Dearly Departing* (2012).

enabled me to take a month away from my business with no repercussions.

Morning working

I've been a morning person all my life. I credit this to my dad, as he was a morning person as well. As a child I never could quite understand why every time I went downstairs, no matter how early, my dad would always be up and around. Mornings work for me, especially around 4am. It's funny, because even Matthew was born at 4am!

4am has been my golden time throughout my life, because at that time, I have this sort of natural body clock that springs into action. I am the most creative person I can ever be. It's peaceful and quiet at 4am – no one is around. You're there, the internet is great because no one is on it, you don't receive many emails or phone calls at 4am and you've got no staff disturbing you. It is between 4am and 7am that I get the most work done. I basically run my business in those three hours of the day. I was therefore delighted when I came across a book devoted to mornings called *The Miracle Morning* by Hal Elrod.[31]

---

[31] H. Elrod, *The Miracle Morning: The 6 Habits That Will Transform Your Life Before 8am* (2017).

I find that routines help me to cope and if you incorporate the following into your day it does really help to reduce stress.

Sleep

I'm lucky in that I can survive effectively on very little sleep. I bounce back all the time and have limitless energy and enthusiasm. I do however love a siesta and will often take a 20-minute power nap at least once a day.

Meditation

I have found meditating for just 10 minutes every day to be critical for survival (I recommend the 10 Minute Mind® programme by Monique Rhodes; www.the10minutemind.com). I am a lot calmer and more thoughtful in my actions as a result. I need to ensure that I make time and prioritise deep breathing and yoga; I've also recently discovered Tension & Trauma Release Exercises (TRE) (www.traumaprevention.com) which I find really helpful for reducing tension and stress. I have trained myself to view meditation and relaxation as important as work and ensure that I have at least one hour a day for myself to focus on these areas.

Visualisation

It is essential that you know where you are heading – I change my vision board on a yearly basis and constantly review my progress against it. I love going to fortune tellers, tarot readers and anyone which will predict my future; I regularly use Angel Cards too. I am a huge believer in the Law of Attraction (www.thelawofattraction.com/what-is-the-law-of-attraction).

Journaling

I wish I had done this better as writing this book would have been a lot easier. I do try to maintain a gratitude journal of three things I'm grateful for every day, and if you are at the beginning of your entrepreneurial journey I would urge you to purchase a really nice business journal to document your journey for when you write your future book!

Reading

Reading is my favourite pastime – I will never go anywhere without a book and I take several on holiday with me.

Learning and personal development

I absolutely love constantly learning; in fact I am passionate about it. However, I've now realised that I really do need to stop this endless quest for personal development and put a stop to the 'shiny-object' syndrome. I often find I know more than the trainers and I need to slow down, listen, implement what I already know and believe I already know enough. I need to realise on a conscious and subconscious level that I am enough.

Diet and exercise

Sadly I've sacrificed my health for the sake of my business, so please don't make this mistake. As soon as I have written this book my attention will turn to my health. There is no way I can hold a book launch looking like I do at the moment. I am currently pre-diabetic and have to do everything I can to reverse this. I struggle to lose weight (because I love food too much), but I also realise that my weight problems stem more from me working too many hours and not putting aside enough time to prepare and plan my meals or exercise. I am at present working with a health coach who is helping me to eat more slowly and mindfully to help my health and to follow intuitive eating which will help with weight loss. Let's see the results at my book launch!

I used to think of exercise as a waste of time, but now I am reaping the benefits of a daily walk with our pet dog Maxy and have also taken up yoga and pilates and engaged the services of a personal trainer. I have also taken up running. However, my favourite exercise is still to walk Maxy up the hill behind the farm – a constant 30 minute climb to the top while listening to a podcast, and when I reach the top there is a rock which I sit down on and just spend 5–10 minutes meditating and feeling grateful, before walking back down again.

Spa days and treatments

I have to have regular massages and spa days (at least once a month) just to cope.

I think that my reflection and my qualifications in stress management have taught me that being an entrepreneur has been far more stressful than anything I experienced in the NHS period of my life. But the difference is that when you're employed by somebody else and in a stressful situation, you think only they are going to benefit. When you're working and you're stressed for yourself, you will be the ultimate beneficiary and it will get better. My work also never actually feels like work as I love it too much – it's a passion which makes me leap out of bed every day and keeps me happy.

In business you learn from the pain, cock-ups and humiliation – this is how you grow and learn. Those people who succeed have drive and the ability to adapt and change as they go along their business journey. Some people are not happy with their lives but they are never willing to change and they will end up on their death bed with regrets.

Bronnie Ware, an Australian palliative care nurse, recorded her experiences with dying patients and summarised common themes which emerged again and again when people were lying on their death bed. Her findings were documented in her book, *The Top Five Regrets of the Dying*:

'I wish I'd had the courage to live a life true to myself, not the life others expected of me.' This is the most common regret of all. When people realise that their life is almost over and look back clearly on it, it is easy to see how many dreams have gone unfulfilled.

'I wish I hadn't worked so hard.' Patients regretted spending so much of their lives on the treadmill of a work existence.

'I wish I'd had the courage to express my feelings.' Many people suppressed their feelings in order to keep peace with others. As a result they settled for a mediocre existence and never became who they were truly capable of becoming.

'I wish I had stayed in touch with my friends.' There were so many deep regrets about not giving friendships the time and effort that they deserved. Everyone misses their friends when they are dying.

'I wish that I had let myself be happier.' – Many did not realise until the end that happiness is a choice. Life is a choice, It is YOUR life. Choose consciously, choose wisely, choose honestly. Choose happiness.[32]

---

[32] B. Ware, 'Regrets of the dying' [blog]. Available from https://bronnieware.com/blog/regrets-of-the-dying/

So what is your bow tie on a llama? What are you going to do to change your life?

Over to you...

- What are (or are going to be) your personal survival tactics?
- If taking a month off work was one of your goals in life, what do you need to do in your business for you to achieve that goal?
- Has your health suffered at the expense of your business?
- Have your relationships been affected due to your business and your style of working?
- Do you have any daily routines which you use to help you cope?

Sources of further support

You don't need to be a genius or a visionary, or even a college graduate for that matter, to be successful. You just need a framework and a dream.

Michael Dell, founder of Dell

Throughout the book I reference various sources of support and further information. These are listed below and the actual resources can also be found on the supporting website to this book: www. celiagaze.com

Chapter 2: What's the crazy idea?

- Phil Knight, *Shoe Dog: A Memoir by the Creator of Nike* (2016)
- New Economics Foundation, *Five Ways to Wellbeing: New Applications, New Ways of Thinking* (2011). Available from: https://neweconomics.org/2011/07/ five-ways-well-new-applications-new-ways-thinking

Chapter 3: How do you begin to transform your premises?

- www.MyBuilder.com – the website I used to obtain quotes for builders
- A Health and Safety Construction Plan, available from the online resources
- Architect in the House scheme
- www.localarchitectsdirect.co.uk – a website you can use to find architects
- Planning portal: www.planningportal.co.uk/applications
- Fire regulations: www.hse.gov.uk/event-safety/fire-safety. htm
- Noise regulations: www.hse.gov.uk/event-safety/noise. htm
- Business rates:www.gov.uk/introduction-to-business-rates
- Challenging your business rates: www.gov.uk/correct-your-business-rates

Chapter 4: It's a numbers game – the importance of cash flow

- Alejandro Cremades, The Art of Startup Fundraising (2016)
- RDPE grant funding: www.gov.uk/rural-development-programme-for-england

- Gino Wickman, *Traction: Get a Grip on Your Business* (2011).
- Access to Finance: www.a2fnw.co.uk
- Understanding VAT: https://entrepreneurhandbook.co.uk/understanding-vat/ and www.gov.uk/vat-businesses
- Brief to recruit my accountant (see online resources)
- Graphical forecasting information I use (see online resources)
- Xero: www.xero.com/uk
- ReceiptBank: www.receipt-bank.com
- Profit First: www.profitfirstbook.com
- Budgeting (see online resources)

Chapter 5: Business processes and systems – how to ensure your venture will be a success

- Gino Wickman, *Traction: Get a Grip on Your Business* (2011).
- Jacqui Mann, *Recruit, Inspire & Retain: How to Create a Company Culture to Grow Your Business* (2018).
- Food Standards Agency: www.food.gov.uk
- Department of Health, Industry Guide 2018.
- Health and Safety Executive: www.hse.gov.uk/catering
- Federation of Small Businesses: www.fsb.org.uk
- How people can smuggle alcohol into your venue (see online resources)

- National Counter Terrorism Security Office/Business Continuity Institute/London First, *Expecting the Unexpected: Business Continuity in an Uncertain World* (2003).
- Information Commissioner's Office, Guide to the General Data Protection Regulation (GDPR) (2018).
- Donald Miller, *Building a Story Brand* (2017). See also: www.storybrand.com
- Bernadette Jiwa, *Difference: The One-Page Method for Reimagining Your Business and Reinventing Your Marketing* (2014). See also: www.difference.is/ difference-map

Chapter 6: Finding, marketing and selling to customers

- Event Temple (venue management software): www. eventtemple.com
- Entrepreneurs Circle: entrepreneurscircle.org
- Nigel Botterill: www.nigelbotterill.com
- Net Promoter Score: www.netpromoter.com/know
- Wedding Biz Club: http://weddingbizclub.com
- BombBomb: https://bombbomb.com
- You Can Book Me: https://youcanbook.me
- The first ever photoshoot undertaken at the farm: https://bridesupnorth.com/2013/10/21/ COUNTRY-LIFE-VINTAGE-GOWNS-

GLORIOUS-TIARAS-FOR-A-STYLED-
BRIDAL-SHOOT-IN-THE-NORTH-WEST/

Chapter 7: Wise up – overcoming staff issues and barriers and becoming resilient

- Innocent Drinks, *A Book about Innocent: Our Story and Some Things We've Learned* (2009).
- Umair Haque, 'The Awesomeness Manifesto', *Harvard Business Review* (16 September 2009). Available from: https://hbr.org/2009/09/is-your-business-innovative-or

Chapter 8: Yes, it can all get out of control...

- James Cox, 'It's all in the positioning: What to do when your business seems to be losing focus', *SmallBusiness* (26 June 2014). Available from: https://smallbusiness. co.uk/its-all-in-the-positioning-what-to-do-when-your-business-seems-to-be-losing-focus-2465692/

Chapter 9: How do you know your crazy idea will work? Being brave

- Carrie Green, *She Means Business: Turn Your Ideas into Reality and Become a Wildly Successful Entrepreneur* (2017).

- Adam Kirk Smith, *The Bravest You: 5 Steps to Fight Your Biggest Fears, Find Your Passion, and Unlock Your Extraordinary Life* (2017).
- Chamber of Commerce: www.britishchambers.org.uk
- Access to Finance: www.a2fnw.co.uk
- Licensing events: www.gov.uk/temporary-events-notice

Chapter 10: The skills you will need to develop to survive

- Gary Keller with Jay Papasan, *The One Thing: The Surprisingly Simple Truth Behind Extraordinary Results* (2014).
- Peter Awad's Go Slow To Grow: peterawad.com
- Jocelyn R. Davis and Tom Atkinson, 'Need Speed? Slow Down'. *Harvard Business Review* (May 2010). Available from: https://hbr.org/2010/05/need-speed-slow-down
- Nigel Botterill and Martin Gladdish, *Building Your Business in 90 Minutes a Day* (2015).

Chapter 11 – How your crazy idea can grow a bigger life

- Hal Elrod, *The Miracle Morning: The 6 Habits That Will Transform Your Life Before 8am* (2017).
- Bronnie Ware, *The Top Five Regrets of the Dying: A Life Transformed by the Dearly Departing* (2012).

You can find further information on The Wellbeing Farm at www.thewellbeingfarm.co.uk

My final story

One of my best moments personally was when I got my puppy, Maxy, at the end of June 2018. I'd always wanted a dog, but Stephen was adamant he didn't want one. So I had to sneakily get a Cairn Terrier, as this was Stephen's favourite breed of dog and he had previously owned one. I thought the only way that Stephen would come around was if I bought a Cairn Terrier. So Matthew and I went against Stephen's advice – I've always been a bit of a rebel that way – and Maxy arrived.

I probably chose the world's most enthusiastic dog. Talk about a dog copying his owner! Maxy has developed all my characteristics: boisterous, energetic, enthusiastic and playful. He doesn't stop. In October 2018, we took him to The Family Pet Show in EventCity in Manchester. For those of you who have never been to EventCity, it's a great big convention complex for meetings and exhibitions right next to the famous Trafford Centre in Manchester. At this point Maxy had not really met other dogs before and he was really thrown in at the deep end – being a family pet show there were dogs of all sizes and pets of all descriptions. You walk and walk, and there are so many stands, so for a new puppy owner like me who needs to get as many outfits as she can for this puppy, it is a shopper's paradise. I was exhausted and sat down with Maxy while Matthew went and played on this double-decker play bus. As Matthew started climbing down the stairs off the bus, I spotted a huge crowd around the dog arena. I thought, oh my goodness, there must be special dog activity going on. So not wanting to miss out, I grabbed Maxy with all the shopping and Matthew and I followed the crowd. I didn't quite know where we were going, so we ended up going through the entrance of a show ring.

Now, I don't know if you've ever seen a dog show like Crufts on television, but it was huge. The showroom was massive. And there I was with my puppy and all these shopping bags. We had entered the show ring, and I tried to turn around but all I faced was an avalanche of dogs and their owners coming through the gate. There was no chance I could turn around and go, 'Oh, sorry, I'm in the wrong place.' Matthew was asking, 'Mummy, where on earth are we going?' And I said, 'Matthew just follow the crowd, we'll have to get into the show and then we'll just walk around the ring and hopefully we can get to the other side and sneak out.'

So I followed the crowd and started walking around but no, my plan wasn't going to work, because everybody stopped walking and turned to face the middle of the show ring. There I was in the official Family Pet Dog Show. This was the first time I'd ever owned a dog. I'd only watched Crufts a couple of times. I hadn't done my hair or make-up, never mind Maxy – I hadn't even brushed him. I was in the middle of a dog show surrounded by all these people preening and pruning their puppies and dogs of all sizes. There I was with a load of shopping, looking very scruffy with my puppy and Matthew.

I had to go along with it. Matthew was going, 'Mummy, what shall we do?' I said 'Be quiet, and go along with it.' So, the celebrity judge starts walking around and when he came to me he said, 'Oh, well who do we have here?' and all I could think to say was, 'Well, this is Maxy my puppy and he's a brand new puppy and I thought the best way to get him to meet other dogs was to bring him to The Family Pet Show.' Now at this point Maxy was shattered, and he was so tired that he literally just sat there. The judge commented on how calm and relaxed Maxy was with all these other dogs around him. So I really just had to go along with it and say 'Thank you very much.' And, 'Yes I believe it's a good way of letting him meet other dogs.'

After that, I thought right, I'll try and escape. So we had to walk around a bit more and then stop, and the judges moved to the middle of the arena and said, 'Thank very much everybody. We've made our decision, and we are now down to the final seven dogs.' Now bear in mind that there were about 70 dogs in this show ring. 'And the final seven are…' and they proceeded to read out a list of dog names and then they pointed at me. I thought they were actually pointing at somebody else, but then they read out 'the Cairn Terrier Maxy'. I nearly died. Oh my goodness, I was no longer going to be able to get away with this. I had not registered for the show; all I had done was follow the crowd into the ring and here I was in the final of The Fun Dog Show at The Family Pet Show.

Can you imagine? I had to walk into the centre of this ring surrounded by 70 other dogs, and a big crowd of dog loving fans. What on earth was I going to say? The seven of us had to line up with our dogs and the judges began doing a full examination. I was asked what my registration number was. Now at this point, what would you do? Do the walk of shame across the ring, faced with a crowd of angry, hostile people because I had robbed them of a place in the dog show final. Or to go along with it and say, 'Oh my goodness, my badge sticker must have got caught in my hair.' (I have got long red hair.) 'I'm so sorry, my badge has fallen off and I just don't know where it's gone. I can't for the life of me remember my registration number.' I'm ashamed to say that I had to go along with the latter, because I was too afraid to do the walk of shame.

While the judges were making their decision, a podium was being set up for the first, second and third placed dogs. Matthew was standing by my side looking absolutely horrified and worried and not knowing what to say. The bags were still at the side of the room, with our coats and everything else thrown onto the floor.

The dogs were announced, in order. In third place, in second place and finally the winner of The Family Pet Show, the dog that the judges would most like to take home is… the Cairn Terrier, Maxy. I was so embarrassed. I hustled Matthew onto the podium; there was no way I was going to be photographed! Matthew sat there with Maxy, who was still being a little angel at this point, and he was the winner of The Family Pet Show.

Figure 12.1: Matthew and Maxy on the podium after winning the 'Dog the judges would most like to take home' award at the Fun Dog Show

He ended up with a load of prizes and to this day I still haven't touched them because I was sure for a long time that I was going to hear a knock at the door and it would be the people who run the pet show asking for them back. I am sorry to everybody who genuinely did enter, because it was a genuine mistake. I never realised I was in a pet show and I'm very sorry for what I did.

The whole purpose of this book has been how to stand out in a crowd, but the moral of the story is sometimes you do have to follow the crowd in order to stand out.

9 781788 601245